D1587727

HERITAGE RAILWAYS
OF THE
BRITISH ISLES

HERITAGE RAILWAYS

OF THE

BRITISH ISLES

INDEX

ANTHONY LAMBERT

This edition first published in 1999 for Index

Henson Way
Kettering
Northants NN16 8PX

© 1999 Brown Packaging Books Ltd

All rights reserved. No part of this publication may be reproduced,
stored in a retrieval system or transmitted, in any form or by any means, electronic,
mechanical, photocopying, recording or otherwise, without the prior written
permission of the copyright holder.

ISBN: 1-84013-288-4

Printed in Singapore

Editorial and design by
Amber Books Ltd
Bradley's Close
74–77 White Lion Street
London N1 9PF

Project Editor: Brian Burns
Design: Hawes Design
Picture Research: Samantha Nunn

CONTENTS

INTRODUCTION

Few letters to **The Times** *can have had such an impact as the first suggestion in 1950 that a meeting be held to develop the idea of preserving a railway. In the subsequent half-century, heritage railways have become a major part of the tourism industry. They are also a tribute to the exceptional capacity of the British for Herculean voluntary effort in a common cause.*

◀ *The line on which it all started: the successful effort to save the Talyllyn Railway in 1950 was the inspiration for railway preservation schemes throughout the world.*

▲ *The charm of the narrow gauge: Isle of Man Railway No 10 G.H. Wood approaches the tiny platform at Ballabeg. Sixteen similar engines once operated on the island.*

◂Some preservation schemes have failed or had to be modified, like the Dart Valley Railway, which was forced to quit Ashburton, seen here in 1970, because of the A38 widening.

There can have been few more portentous meetings for the future of tourism in Britain than the gathering of a group of disparate individuals at the Imperial Hotel in Birmingham in 1950. They were there to discuss saving the Talyllyn Railway, following the sudden death of Sir Henry Haydn Jones, the man who kept the ramshackle railway going against all odds. As Tom Rolt, one of the people present, put it: 'The novel idea of forming a voluntary society to run a public railway was considered crack-brained.'

The success of the Talyllyn Railway Preservation Society (TRPS) has since spawned hundreds of schemes, many of which, in the tradition of the 'Railway Manias' of the 19th century, have fallen by the wayside. But there are now over a hundred major railway lines and centres, and the largest are substantial businesses with a turnover in seven figures. The tourist map of Britain would be immeasurably poorer without them.

Most projects have been started by groups of like-minded individuals trying to save something that they loved and did not want to see disappear. The choice of line has often been a major part of the motivation: for the pioneers of the TRPS, it was a railway line of exceptional character that prompted their endeavours. For others it has been the fascination of the rural branch line; or of the railway to the seaside, redolent of childhood memories of excursion trains, moquette warmed by the sun and the smell of Welsh coal and steam wafting in through the strap-hung window. Often the focus has been the steam engine itself – though many regard locomotives as beautiful even in repose, they have to be seen in action to understand their full appeal.

The varying rationales behind saving a particular locomotive, carriage or railway have helped to create a wonderful diversity of heritage railways. Some railways are long enough to be able to restore each of their stations to a different period. Some favour the pre-grouping era (before 1923, when over a hundred railways were grouped into the 'big four' of the Great Western, London Midland & Scottish, London & North Eastern and Southern railways), when liveries were at their most colourful and first-class carriages at their most sumptuous. Others favour the post-grouping years before nationalization of the railways in

1948, perhaps because they have a preponderance of locomotives and rolling stock from that period. A few re-create the first decade or so of British Railways, the swan song of steam and lined locomotives.

If this book testifies to anything, it is to the immense capacity of the British people for voluntary activity. Nowhere else has the heritage railway been developed on anything like the same scale, though the concept has been emulated throughout the world. As railways have grown, it has been necessary to take on some paid staff, but there is hardly a railway that could last without volunteer help. Assistance has come from other quarters, too. Various job training schemes set up by the government have enabled many projects to be tackled, to the benefit of both the railway and the participants, who have developed useful skills. The armed services have also been a constant source of help, often adopting as a training exercise a particular project such as a bridge reconstruction.

The dependence on volunteer support is obviously a source of anxiety for railway managers. There can be differences of opinion over spending priorities between the commercial imperatives of the business and the preservation instincts of the volunteers. More intractable is the question of whether steam railways will hold their fascination for generations that have grown up in the computer age, and if there will still be sufficient volunteers to run the labour-intensive railways, some of which require a staff running into three figures on busy days in the summer. The signs are that the steam locomotive and heritage railways have lost none of their appeal: passenger figures are holding up on most lines at a time when some other tourist attractions are suffering a downturn in business. Sunday trading has done nothing to help either visitor figures in the tourist industry as a whole or the availability of volunteers.

To help broaden the appeal and commercial base of heritage railways, most offer more than rides. Naturally a buffet or tea room and a shop are indispensable adjuncts of any tourist operation, but many railways

Major construction projects have been undertaken by heritage railways. The signal box controlling Kidderminster station on the Severn Valley was built from scratch to GWR design.

also operate trains that offer lunch or dinner, exploiting the perennial appeal of eating while a panorama rolls past the window. 'Wine and dine' trains offer a high standard of cuisine and are often booked up months ahead.

Equally well-subscribed are the engine-driving courses that some railways operate on weekdays or quieter weekends. These last from half a day to several days, and range from puffing up and down a yard to driving a train over the full length of the line. All are preceded by instruction on safety matters and operating procedures, and many involve the full range of tasks involved in preparing a steam engine for work, such as steam raising and taking on water, and disposing of an engine at the end of the day.

Santa specials attract hundreds of thousands of visitors and provide a vital income boost during the normally quiet months between early October and Easter. The usual offering is a ride to Santa's grotto (or Santas' grottos on the busier lines), with a present for the children while the grown-ups get a mince pie and mulled wine.

Throughout the operating season, most railways offer a range of special weekends. A 'Thomas the Tank Engine' weekend is probably the most universal. Other common themes include gatherings of commercial vehicles and traction engines; 1940s weekends, when the railway takes on a wartime appearance; heavy horse weekends; and diesel and steam galas that entail running demonstration freight trains, double-heading and other activities.

Looking to the future, the number of lines continues to grow, though at nothing like the rate of the past three decades. The 17.6-km (11-mile) line between Keith and Dufftown in Morayshire is expected to reopen soon, taking advantage of its mothballed status since freight traffic ended in 1991. This may facilitate access to distilleries for freight traffic, another area that is likely to develop as English Welsh & Scottish Railway wins more traffic back to rail. Contract engineering work has emerged as a useful source of income for the larger lines with well-equipped workshops, as has engine leasing for those in

the fortunate position of having more working locomotives than needed for the scheduled services.

Another growing trend is the use of heritage railways as a means of transport. As road traffic continues to grow, railways that can play a part in alleviating congestion are receiving official

♦Chartered specials for photographers often re-create a particular period with authentic locomotive and rolling stock. LNER B12/3 No 8572 and teak stock at Foley Park on the Severn Valley.

encouragement and investment from local authorities. Examples are the East Lancashire Railway, Keighley & Worth Valley Railway, Kent & East Sussex Railway, North Yorkshire Moors Railway, and Swanage Railway at Corfe Castle. In contrast, the negative attitude by some parties towards the traffic-reduction potential of the Welsh Highland Railway is bewildering.

Two areas that are underdeveloped are the educational potential of heritage railways and corporate entertainment – especially where facilities can be provided for seminars and meetings, as at the Kidderminster Railway Museum/Severn Valley Railway.

Heritage railways are now a well-established part of the tourism industry in Britain. They receive over 7.8 million visitors a year and have a combined turnover in excess of £43 million. Their total distance, irrespective of gauge (683km/427 miles), is greater than the distance between London and Glasgow, and they are served by 570 stations – more than twice the number on the London Underground.

How to use this book

This book is a guide to railways rather than to preservation centres. The principal criterion for inclusion is that a railway takes visitors from A to B on the preserved route or reconstructed trackbed of a former railway, rather than round in a circle as on many miniature railways.

The period of operation is intended as a rough guide: timetables are adjusted from year to year, so it is

◀ *The workshops on the Bluebell Railway illustrate the scale of engineering work required to maintain steam locomotives, supplemented by specialist engineering companies.*

ABBREVIATIONS

Cadw	*Welsh equivalent of English Heritage*
EH	*English Heritage*
NT	*National Trust*
NTS	*National Trust for Scotland*

wise to obtain an up-to-date timetable before making a visit.

For obvious reasons, the railway is not an easy environment in which to cater for the disabled, especially regarding access to areas normally denied to passengers on Railtrack. However, many railways have done their utmost to make such visits possible. Special toilets are available on most railways, some have special coaches and others have ramps to aid wheelchair access. It is always best to telephone before a visit.

➤ *The South Eastern & Chatham Railway family saloon coach on the Kent & East Sussex Railway illustrates the quality of early carriages, which require special skills for restoration.*

CHAPTER 1
SOUTH &
SOUTH-EAST
ENGLAND

Standard gauge railway preservation may be said to have begun in this

region when, in 1960, the Bluebell Railway began regular passenger services

between Sheffield Park and Horsted Keynes.

◀On the Kent & East Sussex Railway, the South Eastern & Chatham Railway P class 0-6-0 tank No. 1556 of 1909 is seen with a mixed train typical of pre-preservation operation.

◆One of the USA 0-6-0 tanks imported during the Second World War, which became BR No 30064, waits to leave the attractive station at Sheffield Park on the Bluebell Railway.

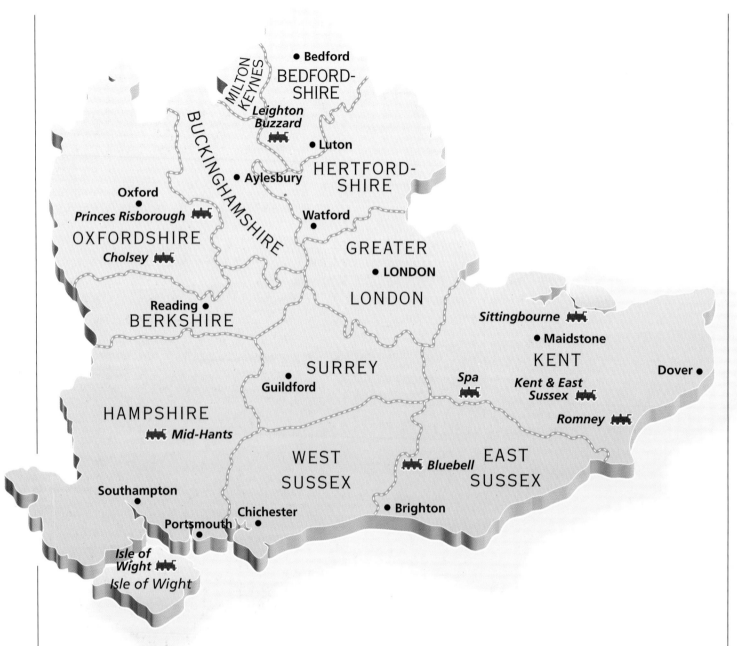

BLUEBELL RAILWAY

It is no wonder that the Bluebell Railway is one of the best-known preserved railways, for it is the oldest of Britain's standard gauge heritage railways, opening its carriage doors for the first time on 7 August 1960. It is a measure of its longevity that in January 2000 the railway will have been in the same ownership for longer than any of its previous owners.

Even before it opened to visitors the Bluebell line was a household name because it had become a national symbol of resistance to the railway closures that were beginning to take place in the years leading up to the wholesale slaughter of the Beeching years. Unusually on this occasion it was an individual who compelled British Railways (BR) to reopen the line after it had been closed in May 1955.

A local resident named Miss Bessemer discovered that the Act of Parliament transferring ownership from the fledgling Lewes & East Grinstead Railway (L&EGR) to the London Brighton & South Coast Railway (LBSCR), which completed and opened the line in 1882, conferred an obligation to operate at least four trains a day. This requirement was legally passed on through ownership changes, so BR had to reopen the line, which happened in August 1956.

Although this episode generated a national debate about whether valuable public services should be subsidized, it did not save the Bluebell line and services were finally withdrawn on 16 March 1958. None the less, this stay of execution, coupled with the national prominence given to the line, encouraged proposals to reopen it as a preserved railway. Inspired by the example of the Talyllyn and the Festiniog, a preservation society was formed and began to negotiate with BR for the section between Sheffield Park and Horsted Keynes.

There is a world of difference between preserving narrow gauge lines of obvious charm running through popular holiday areas and attempting to save a standard gauge railway, with its much higher costs, running through a quiet if pretty part of Sussex. There were no precedents to indicate that the general public would warm to the idea of a ride on a preserved steam

railway as a day out. Thankfully for railway enthusiasts and the tourist industry of Britain, the Bluebell Railway proved very popular and its success helped to bring dozens of other railways into being.

A major reason for the popularity of the Bluebell line is the lovely countryside through which it passes. Most passengers begin their journey at Sheffield Park, named after the nearby country house, whose 19th-century owner, Lord Sheffield, was chairman of the L&EGR. This once-quiet country station is now the locomotive headquarters of the railway, with a workshop and running-shed building designed to reflect LBSCR architectural features.

This attention to detail is a hallmark of the Bluebell Railway, which is greatly admired by railway

➥ *Southern Railway U class 2-6-0 No 1618 with a winter working. This was only the second locomotive to be rescued from the scrapyard at Barry.*

◆*Among the most opulent of railway carriages are Pullman Cars, of which the Bluebell has four. Note the inlay around the clock on the Pullman Car* **Fingall** *of 1924.*

◆*Another view of the inlay on* **Fingall,** *which was used on the* **Bournemouth Belle** *during the 1950s. It has a kitchen and seats for 22 people.*

enthusiasts for the way it has refused to indulge in the 'Disneyfication' of locomotives and carriages, setting greater store on historical accuracy than on whimsy. The Bluebell takes the view that the innate charm of

the English country railway, when well-presented, is of greater and more enduring appeal than spurious liveries and toy-town trimmings.

In the restoration of its stations, the Bluebell has cleverly chosen a progression in time that begins with Sheffield Park, where the elegant station by T W Myres has been restored as it would have looked in about 1900. A welcoming fire burns in the booking-hall grate in cool weather, and the ting of signalling instrument bells and the crash of signal levers may be heard from the platform signal box as you buy your ticket.

Leaving Sheffield Park, trains cross the River Ouse and pass a particularly fine LBSCR bracket signal on the right. The engine soon has to get down to business, for the line rises at a gradient of 1 in 75 up Freshfield Bank, through well-treed, rolling countryside to Lindfield Wood, one of several areas that are covered with bluebells in spring. A cutting leads to the impressive Three Arch Bridge over the line as it climbs up the last stretch into Horsted Keynes, heralded by large carriage sheds on the right. On the left may be glimpsed the remnants of the line that led south-west towards Haywards Heath and Brighton, followed by the large signal box that controlled the junction.

The intermediate station at Horsted Keynes offers visitors the appearance of a busy country junction of the 1930s. Few preserved stations can produce the ambience of a bygone era as well as Horsted Keynes: its seclusion and rural setting banish thoughts of a new

BLUEBELL RAILWAY

Length of line: *14.1km (9 miles)*
Operating periods:
Weekends throughout the year; daily May–September and school holidays; Bank Holidays.
Facilities:
Restaurant, buffet, bar, shops, museum, depot, Pullman lunch trains.
Access for disabled:
Ramps for access to trains; special toilets at Sheffield Park and Kingscote.
Public transport:
Bus No 473 from East Grinstead station (Connex) connects all Bluebell trains.
Nearby tourist attractions:
Sheffield Park Garden (NT), Standen (NT), Priest House (West Hoathly, EH).
Address:
Sheffield Park Station, Uckfield, East Sussex TN22 3QL.
Telephone (information): *01825 722008*
Telephone (timetable): *01825 722370*

millennium, and a comparison between historic pictures and the scene today shows that remarkably little has changed in 70 years. The junction was grand enough to warrant a subway linking the platforms and long canopies along the platforms. Sitting in the island platform's cosy period bar when the sun sets on an October afternoon, as the warm glow of the lamps replaces daylight, it is easy to imagine what it would have been like waiting for a connecting train when it was still possible to catch a train down to Haywards Heath and Brighton.

Continuing northwards over the new extension, opened in stages between June 1990 and April 1994, the train passes a row of white railway cottages on the left and soon the spire of Highbrook church comes into view on the left. Views across open country contract as the line passes under one of the line's few stone structures, a bridge near Horsted House Farm, before entering Courtland Wood and plunging into the longest tunnel on a British preserved railway. West Hoathly Tunnel is straight, rather damp and 668m (2193ft) long.

The train passes the site of West Hoathly station and clatters over the new steel bridge that the Bluebell had to erect over the road to Coombe Farm – its predecessor was dismantled after the railway closed. An open section is followed by a sandstone cutting before dropping down a gentle gradient to the current northern terminus at Kingscote. The station here completes the successive advances in the period chosen for restoration, having a 1950s flavour.

A planning condition of the railway's reinstatement, because of an understandable reluctance to despoil the area with parking, was that access to Kingscote station should be by public transport only – leading to the daft situation where the railway has to turn away walkers and cyclists. A bus service, often operated by a vintage bus, links Kingscote with East Grinstead

British Railways-built Standard Class 5 4-6-0 Camelot was built in 1955 and delivered to Bluebell in October 1979. It is seen here on its way from Sheffield Park to Kingscote. Note the bluebells in the foreground.

◄British Railways Class 4MT 4-6-0 No 75027 leaves Horsted Keynes with a permanent way train for West Hoathly. Horsted Keynes is a rare example in preservation of a classic country junction.

station (route 473) and through tickets for the Bluebell and the bus can be purchased from any Connex South Central station.

In due course, the line will be extended beyond Kingscote to link up with Railtrack at East Grinstead, which will greatly simplify access to the Bluebell by public transport.

One of the greatest advantages that the infant Bluebell Railway enjoyed was the remarkable variety of historic locomotives and rolling stock still in service on BR. Despite limited funds and difficult choices, the railway did well in saving from the cutter's torch a good selection of 19th- and early 20th-century locomotives and carriages. As a result, only two or three other railways can match the antiquity and interest of the Bluebell's smaller engines. The pioneers chose small engines not only because they were cheaper to buy and run, but also because no one at that time could conceive of the need for sufficient power to haul trains of more than three or four coaches.

The majority of the Bluebell's locomotives are from the Southern Railway and its pre-grouping constituents, with a few British Railways' designs that worked over Southern Region lines. Among the early gems are a pair of LBSCR Terrier 0-6-0 tank engines with the very unrural names of *Fenchurch* and *Stepney*, which date from 1872 and 1875 respectively, 0-6-2T *Birch Grove* of 1898 and the handsome South Eastern & Chatham Railway H class 0-4-4T of 1905. At the other end of the scale are a pair of Bulleid Pacifics built for express workings and one of the huge 2-10-0 freight engines that was the last class of steam locomotive to be built in Britain.

Part of the pleasure of a journey over a preserved railway is sitting in a vehicle very different from a coach on a HST 125 or a London commuter train. The Bluebell was fortunate enough to secure 13 pre-First World War passenger carriages and another 12 inter-war vehicles. Restored to a very high standard by volunteers, these carriages help to re-create the experience of train travel of various decades during the past century.

CHINNOR & PRINCES RISBOROUGH RAILWAY

Many preserved railways have been able to develop a role in feeding traffic to the national network, or encouraging passengers to use trains to visit them. In an increasing number of cases this has involved freight traffic, but the Chinnor & Princes Risborough Railway (CPRR) is the subject of one of the most ambitious schemes to date.

At present the terminus of the line from Princes Risborough is Chinnor, once an intermediate station on the Great Western Railway (GWR) branch to Watlington. By relaying the railway on the old trackbed to the site of Aston Rowant station, the line would be within a stone's throw of the M40, creating the possibility of a park-and-ride station for the area. This would be served by Chiltern Railways' services out of Marylebone. There is no prospect of this happening until the first decade of the 21st century, but such projects may well be the salvation of some marginal preserved railways.

The 19th-century Watlington & Princes Risborough Railway came into being when the Wallingford & Watlington Railway (see p.23) failed to progress to the second town in its title. It opened in 1872, was in financial trouble from the start and was bought by the GWR in 1883 for less than half the cost of construction.

By the mid-1950s passenger receipts were so low that closure was proposed and took place in 1957. Freight continued to the cement works at Chinnor

---

CHINNOR & PRINCES RISBOROUGH RAILWAY

Length of line: *6.4km (4 miles)*
Operating periods: *Weekends Easter–October.*
Facilities: *Buffet, shop.*
Public transport:
  Wycombe Bus Nos 232, 331 and 332 from Princes Risborough to Chinnor (Saturday only).
Nearby tourist attractions: *Ridgeway Path.*
Address:
  Chinnor Station, Station Road, Chinnor, Oxfordshire OX9 4ER.
Telephone (timetable): *01844 353535*

until British Rail declared the wagons life-expired, the last train running in December 1989. The CPRR took over maintenance of the track, built a new platform at Chinnor, bought the freehold of the line from BR and started running trains on 20 August 1994, gradually extending to the present terminus at Thame Junction on the outskirts of Princes Risborough. It is expected that trains will run into the Railtrack station in due course.

When this happens, the CPRR will be able to control train movements from the largest preserved signal box still on its original site; the Grade II listed box has already been restored.

The line runs parallel with the striking ridge of the Chiltern escarpment through pleasant farmland and close to the villages of Bledlow and Horsenden, which has a manor house and church.

A small collection of rolling stock has been assembled, hauled by one of the three diesel locomotives or the one former colliery steam locomotive, built in 1952 and named *Sir Robert Peel*.

➤ *Visiting GWR 0-6-0 pannier tank No 1638 recreates a branch line scene on the Chinnor & Princes Risborough Railway, passing the site of Wainhill Halt on its way to Chinnor.*

CHOLSEY & WALLINGFORD RAILWAY

Among the youngest of the preservation schemes in this book, the Cholsey & Wallingford Railway Preservation Society was founded on the day the last British Rail passenger train ran, 31 May 1981. The train was a special and followed the cessation of malt traffic over the line, the regular passenger service having been withdrawn as long ago as 1959.

One of the shortest of former Great Western Railway (GWR) branch lines, at 5.2km (3¼ miles), the railway was the first standard gauge branch to be built off Brunel's magnificent broad gauge (2140mm/7ft) main line between London Paddington and Bristol. It was built by the independent Wallingford & Watlington Railway but never reached its second destination and was quickly absorbed by the GWR.

From the initial nine return passenger trains a day, the service grew to 19 return workings a day by 1925. It was cut back to 11 a day in 1951 and in June 1959 the last passenger train ran. The line stayed open for freight, and in 1968 British Rail allowed the Great Western Society at Didcot to use the line for a series of special passenger trains using 0-4-2T No 1466 and an auto-coach. The following year the line was truncated at Hithercroft Road so that the bridge and station at Wallingford could be demolished and redeveloped as housing.

Consequently the Cholsey & Wallingford Railway (CWR) is planning to rebuild the terminus in the style of the original station. It has managed to rebuild the railway into the bay platform at Cholsey station originally used by the branch trains, enabling rail-borne visitors to make a simple cross-platform change, and is now running services over the full line.

As a latecomer to preservation, the CWR had little opportunity to acquire steam locomotives that were being discarded by industry, steam on BR having finished long before. An engine is on loan from Guinness Park Royal Brewery and is under restoration, but for immediate services the CWR has to rely on engines borrowed from other railways.

➤*Hunslet 0-6-0 saddle tank No 68006 of 1944 hauls a train towards the main line on the Cholsey & Wallingford Railway. The Leeds-built tank is one of two industrial steam locomotives on the line.*

CHOLSEY & WALLINGFORD RAILWAY

Length of line: *4km (2½ miles)*
Operating periods: *Irregular weekends.*
Facilities: *Coffee shop, shop, museum, model railway.*
Public transport: *Cholsey station (Thames Trains).*
Nearby tourist attractions:
  Didcot Railway Centre,
  Ridgeway Path.
Location:
  Hithercroft Industrial Estate,
  St Johns Road, Wallingford
Address:
  Cholsey & Wallingford Railway Preservation Society,
  PO Box 16, Wallingford,
  Oxfordshire OX10 0NF.
Telephone (timetable): *01491 835067*

▲*Wallingford station with GWR 0-4-2 tank No 1407 shortly before the passenger services were withdrawn on 15 June 1959. The engine shed had been taken out of use in February 1956.*

ISLE OF WIGHT STEAM RAILWAY

Of the many islands off Britain's coastline, the overwhelming majority are home to birds and wildlife rather than to people; only a handful have had a population large enough to justify the construction of railways. Not surprisingly the Isle of Wight is one of them, and the 88-km (55-mile) network that was developed during the 19th century proved a magnet for connoisseurs of vintage railways. Even in the 1960s most of its locomotives and carriages dated from before the First World War.

The longevity of the island's railway equipment was of great benefit to the Isle of Wight Steam Railway (IoWSR), which was set up in the 1960s to preserve a section of the Ryde–Cowes line. This was closed in 1966, the year when steam came to an end on the sole surviving line from Ryde pier to Shanklin with the changeover to electric tube trains imported from the Piccadilly line. Electric services began in 1967. Although still in its infancy, the IoWSR was able to take advantage of the steam locomotives and rolling stock made redundant by the electrification scheme.

As a result, a journey over the line today is as authentic an experience as one is likely to find on any heritage railway. Three of the steam locomotives in its collection worked on the island, and nearly all its coaches date from before the grouping in 1922. Many have been superbly restored with moquette upholstery on the bench seats, a selection of framed railway maps, photographs of picturesque scenes and advertisements that were once mounted above the seats of most railway carriages, and the leather straps that lower the door window.

The best way to visit the IoWSR is by train along the Island Line, changing at the remote platform of

Smallbrook Junction, where in steam days there was nothing but a signal box that was switched out during the winter months. Getting out of a venerable tube train and stepping into a carriage that would have been familiar to Edwardians is a unique juxtaposition.

The line heads off through woods that are a mass of bluebells in spring to reach more open farmland on the approach to Ashey. Until the grandstand burned down in 1929, a racecourse immediately to the south of the line provided a welcome source of revenue for the railway, though the course continued to be used for biannual pony races. The station is not at present in use, but it is hoped to reopen it one day.

After passing through more woodland, the village of Havenstreet comes into view on the right. This was once the home of John Rylands, after whom the famous library in Manchester is named. As an act of

local philanthropy, he built for the village a small gasworks that can be seen on the left as the train runs into Haven Street station (like its predecessors, the IoWSR uses the uncontracted name).

The village is out of sight of the station, which is idyllically rural, though the sole porter-signalman based here had good reason to think it a little too rural – on more than one occasion he entered the tiny signal box to find an adder had paid a visit. Today the station is the headquarters of the railway, with a locomotive and carriage repair shed, and sidings for the railway's collection of over 30 wagons.

➡ *The interior of Haven Street signal box with its 16-lever, knee-high frame, brass signal repeaters to confirm the position of the signal arms on the board above, and on the right a Tyer's token machine.*

◀ *The Isle of Wight Steam Railway terminus at Wootton is a new creation on a different site from the old station. The engine is Terrier 0-6-0 tank No 32640 (formerly W11 Newport).*

A stiff climb of 1 in 66 faces westbound trains from Haven Street, made obvious by passing a rake of carriages in a siding on the left at roof height. The railway bisects an old oak wood and runs through fields of sheep, the engine whistling for a series of gated farm crossings, before arriving at the shaded terminus at Wootton. The original station site was further west, but unstable soil and a landslip prevented its use, compelling the railway to build a new station with items recovered from the island's closed stations – Freshwater provided the small signal box.

In keeping with the island's railway history, the IoWSR's six steam locomotives are all tank engines, because tender engines were never used. Two of them are London Brighton & South Coast Railway 0-6-0 Terrier tanks, No 8 *Freshwater* and No 11 *Newport*, which date from 1876 and 1878 respectively and were both at work on the island before the First World War. The pride of the fleet is from the class of locomotive that was most associated with the island – Adams' pretty Class O2 0-4-4T No 24 *Calbourne*, dating from 1891.

ISLE OF WIGHT STEAM RAILWAY

Length of line: *8km (5 miles)*
Operating periods:
   Daily June–August and most of May and
   September; Sundays in April and October.
Facilities: *Buffet, shop, museum.*
Access for disabled: *Special toilet.*
Public transport:
   Cross-platform change with Island Line trains
   at Smallbrook Junction.
Nearby tourist attractions:
   Robin Hill Country Park,
   Nunwell House and Garden.
Address:
   Haven Street, Ryde,
   Isle of Wight PO33 4DS.
Telephone (information): *01983 882204*

➡ *The charm of the IoWSR line owes much to the carefully re-created character of the stations and the marvellous, almost unmatched, collection of historic carriages.*

◀*Hunslet 'Austerity' 0-6-0 saddle tank No 198* **Royal Engineer** *nears journey's end at Wootton. This class of engine was produced in large numbers during the Second World War.*

April 1900 and was extended up the steep bank to Tenterden Town three years later. The final stretch of track on from Tenterden to Headcorn to connect with the Tonbridge–Ashford main line was opened in 1905.

The KESR held its head above water until the 1920s, when increasing road competition, engendered by the sell-off of ex-services motor chassis by the government, eroded goods traffic and put the railway into receivership. After Stephens's death in 1931, his precarious empire was managed by a former associate, W H Austen, who adopted a more commercial approach, weeding out useless stock and making gradual improvements.

It was during the 1930s that part of the KESR achieved national fame, when one of its locomotives, No 2 *Northiam*, became the star of the Will Hay comedy *Oh! Mr Porter*, for which it was renamed *Gladstone*. During the war the railway had rail-mounted guns patrolling between Rolvenden and Wittersham Road hauled by a Great Western Railway Dean Goods. Soon after the war, the line was nationalized along with the rest of Britain's railways.

British Railways withdrew passenger services over the KESR in January 1954 and lifted the track on the northern section between Headcorn and Tenterden Town the following year. A daily goods train served the southern section and through trains of hop-pickers were run from London in the season. The last train ran on 11 June 1961.

A preservation society was formed and had a much greater struggle than most to bring its plans to fruition, even having to take the transport minister of the day to court. Much of the obstruction stemmed from the road-obsessed transport policy-makers of the day, who objected to a level-crossing on a preserved railway holding up the traffic for a couple of minutes.

Perseverance was rewarded on 3 February 1974, when the first section reopened from Tenterden Town to Rolvenden. This was followed in 1977 by a major extension to Wittersham Road and finally to Northiam, the present terminus, in 1990. The next section, by April 2000, will be to Bodiam, where the late 14th-century castle was a great attraction even before the railway was built and was a major element

KENT & EAST SUSSEX RAILWAY

To appreciate the significance of the Kent & East Sussex Railway (KESR) and its place in railway history, there is no better starting point than the Col. Stephens' Railway Museum. Occupying a building across the level crossing from Tenterden Town station, this superbly laid out museum captures in a series of imaginative displays the eccentric railway empire that the equally eccentric Col. Stephens built up.

The KESR set the pattern for the growth of Col. Stephens' empire of 17 railways, for which he was either managing director, manager or engineer. It was the first of his ventures after passage of the Light Railway Act of 1896, which relieved railways built under the Act of many of the more onerous obligations imposed on a normal railway. This enabled a number of otherwise marginal railways to be constructed and return – in a few cases – a modest profit.

The section of the KESR between the junction with the Tunbridge Wells–Hastings line at Robertsbridge and Rolvenden opened to traffic on 2

KENT & EAST SUSSEX RAILWAY

Length of line: *11.2km (7 miles); 16km (10 miles) from April 2000*

Operating periods:
Weekends April–October; daily July–August, most of June and September, and school holiday weeks.

Facilities:
Buffet, shop, Col. Stephens' Railway Museum.

Access for disabled:
Special coach (please telephone first); toilets at Tenterden and Northiam, and in coach.

Public transport:
Bus No 400 from Ashford station.

Nearby tourist attractions:
Smallhythe Place (NT), Great Dixter.

Address:
Tenterden Town Station, Tenterden, Kent TN30 6HE.

Telephone (information): *01580 765155*

Telephone (timetable): *01580 762943*

♠ *South Eastern & Chatham Railway P class 0-6-0 tank No 1556 of 1909 crosses the Hexden Channel between Wittersham Road and Northiam.*

in passenger projections. The KESR hopes that the castle will boost figures, while the villagers and the National Trust, which owns the castle, will welcome a means of reaching Bodiam without using a car.

Although the preservation society has had to improve the basic and spartan facilities that were characteristic of Col. Stephens' railways, care has been taken not to destroy the 'light railway' atmosphere. The new buildings for passengers at Tenterden Town, for example, have been set back from the platform, while the size of the carriage workshop does not overwhelm the small market-town scale of the station, uniquely built of brick (corrugated iron and wood were used for the others). Col. Stephens would have approved of the source of some additions: the refreshment room is

◀ *In April 2000 the Kent & East Sussex Railway will link Tenterden with Bodiam, where the famous moated late 14th-century castle is in the care of the National Trust.*

a recycled bus station office of 1921 from Maidstone, which was threatened with destruction by road building.

For those with an eye for the finer points of railway architecture, the signal box at Tenterden Town is one of the most pleasing on any preserved railway. Rescued from Chilham on the Ashford–Canterbury line, it is well-proportioned with a pronounced overhang of the eaves and subtle decoration on the barge boards.

The majority of visitors wanting to gain an idea of what the old KESR was like would probably draw the line at the carriages that most passengers once had to endure. In fact, the KESR had some newly built four-wheel carriages when the line opened, but they would still have been fairly spartan. None the less, for those intent on the authentic experience, the KESR has a magnificent train of Victorian vehicles ranging from a four-wheel South Eastern & Chatham Railway (SECR)

A classic mixed train from the age of Col. Stephens, with a London, Brighton & South Coast Railway A1X class 0-6-0 tank No 32678 at the start of the climb from Rolvenden to Tenterden Town.

full third to a six-wheel London & North Western Railway directors' saloon – austerity to opulence.

Most journeys over the line will be made in carriages of the 1930s or 1950s. A couple of puffs from the engine and the train is on a descending gradient that averages 1 in 50 down to Rolvenden but is as steep as 1 in 36, which elicits a vigorous bark from the chimney of ascending locomotives. Furious whistling for the level-crossing over the Ashford–Hastings road heralds the approach to Rolvenden, which was, and still is, the locomotive depot for the line. However, the only original structure is the concrete water tower near the end of the platform.

The marshy nature of the surrounding land is very obvious as the train leaves Rolvenden, one section of the line even being below sea level. A freshwater crayfish farm is passed on the right. The primrose and bluebell carpeted woods are also home to owls and woodpeckers, and swans and herons can be seen around the water course that the railway follows on its way to Wittersham Road. The willow trees that can be seen near the railway were a rather pathetic attempt by Mr Austen to supplement the railway's

▶Col. Stephens' railways were full of character, exemplified by this Shefflex set, consisting of two buses mounted back-to-back. They were so uncomfortable that they drove passengers away.

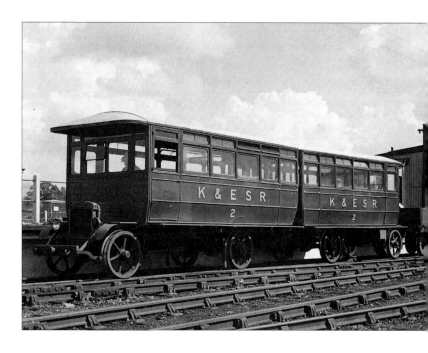

meagre income during the 1930s by selling the wood to cricket-bat makers.

Wittersham Road station is a good example of how many heritage railways have saved buildings that would probably have been destroyed. Many railways have confronted bare ground where once a station stood, so that every platform brick, every lamp and every building had to be found from somewhere else. The quest for at least a railway origin for each item,

➥Two of the KESR's three Terrier A1X 0-6-0 tanks at Tenterden Town: No 10 Sutton and No 32670. At one time the station had an island platform behind the engines.

even if not the 'right' railway (of little account on the KESR anyway), has meant scouring the country for available, suitable artefacts. At Wittersham Road the building came from Borth in North Wales, the signal box from Deal Junction, the signals from Ireland, the railings from Cranbrook and the lamps from Hever and Cowden – all the work of dedicated volunteers.

The village of Wittersham itself lies 4.8km (3 miles) away from the station (hence the word 'Road'). It was once on an island in the English Channel and is still surrounded by marsh. The steep climb out of Wittersham Road station is obvious to the naked eye, causing engines to work hard from a standing start. A short descent follows, taking the train on to a long straight across the Rother Levels and a bridge over the River Rother itself, which marks the county boundary between Kent and East Sussex.

Across the fields is the village of Newenden,

◆ The southern junction of the KESR was on the Tunbridge Wells–Hastings line at Robertsbridge, where A1X 0-6-0 No 3 **Bodiam** *waits in the bay in May 1948.*

▶Within walking distance of Northiam station is the 15th-century manor house of Great Dixter, restored and enlarged in 1910 by Sir Edward Lutyens, who also laid out the garden.

where a small hop-garden survives. A level-crossing precedes arrival at the present terminus of Northiam, where the corrugated-iron station building has been painstakingly restored to near-original condition. The village is a mile or so away and contains the pretty 15th-century hall-house of Great Dixter, which was restored by Lutyens. The house and garden are open to visitors.

Astonishingly, two original KESR locomotives survived long enough to be saved for the railway. The oldest is Terrier 0-6-0 tank No 3 *Bodiam*, which was built by the London Brighton & South Coast Railway in 1872. It has been joined on the railway by two other Terriers. The other native is P class 0-6-0T No 1556, which was built at Ashford in 1909 for the SECR. Most of the other locomotives are also tank engines – the 'light' nature of the line's structures prevents the use of locomotives with high axle weights.

▲*An evening line-up at Page's Park:* **Rishra**, *built in 1921 by E G Baguley of Burton-on-Trent;* **Pixie**, *built by Kerr Stuart in 1922 and last used commercially near Tavistock; and* **Doll**, *a Barclay of 1919.*

LEIGHTON BUZZARD RAILWAY

The extraction of sand has long been a major industry around the Bedfordshire town of Leighton Buzzard, and it is to this industry that the Leighton Buzzard Railway (LBR) owes its existence. Opened in 1919, it was part of an extensive network of 610mm (2ft) gauge lines that linked the quarries with the national railway network. Each of these quarries had its own fleet of small petrol engines that hauled tipper wagons known as 'skips' from the quarry face to an interchange point on the narrow gauge 'main line'. Up to a hundred of these engines could be seen at work within a 3.2-km (2-mile) radius of the town centre, helping to keep 3000 tonnes of sand a week off the roads.

In 1967 the decline of sand traffic gave a group of enthusiasts the opportunity to use the line at weekends, on condition that they undertake some much-needed improvements to the track. In due course they were able to take it over completely when the sand traffic ceased altogether. Quarries are still active, however, as can be seen on the right as soon as the train leaves the main station at Page's Park. A vast crater indicates the scale of the industry, though extraction is now carried out by massive grab excavators.

Page's Park itself, on the north-west side of the line, provides a sylvan setting for the station, providing shade for passengers admiring the locomotive of their train before departure. Visitors can also see the LBR's engine and carriage shed, which stand to the south-east of the station.

The industrial railway that preceded the LBR did not even have workmen's trains, so all the carriages have had to be built by the railway. Some have been built from components derived from War Department

LEIGHTON BUZZARD RAILWAY

Length of line: *4.8km (3 miles)*

Operating periods:

Sundays mid-March–mid-October; Saturdays in August and holiday weekends; Bank Holidays; Wednesdays in June–August; Thursdays in August.

Facilities:

Buffet, shop, depots at Page's Park and Stonehenge.

Access for disabled:

Access to principal buildings, special toilets, wheelchairs on trains.

Public transport:

Leighton Buzzard station, bus to town centre.

Nearby tourist attractions: *Ascott (NT).*

Address:

Page's Park Station, Billington Road, Leighton Buzzard LU7 8TN.

Telephone (information and timetable):

01525 373888

wagons (with some attention to the suspension), others from Polish narrow gauge bogies. Most passengers will not have witnessed the ritual at the ungated level-crossings: in the absence of gates or lights, the red flag-toting guard and fireman stand in the road to stop the odd car. Industrial railways were often allowed dispensation from the requirements of a passenger-carrying railway, and the railway crosses only quiet suburban or country roads.

Today the train creeps through the outskirts of the town past the backs of houses, where there were once fields when the railway was conveying sand. Even before leaving the town behind there are views towards the Chilterns, and various local landmarks can be picked out, such as Ivinghoe Beacon and the Whipsnade chalk lion.

The gradients on the line are steep: the 1 in 25 of Marleys Bank, less than 1.6km (1 mile) from Page's

☛*Bagnall 0-4-0 **Woto** of 1924 was built for Callenders Cables Construction Co. in Erith, Kent. The original 1067-mm (3-ft 6-in) gauge locomotive was converted to 610-mm (2-ft) gauge in 1988–90.*

Park, has locomotives on southbound trains working flat out when the load is heavy. The one passing loop on the line is situated just before Hockcliffe Road; this enables a two-train service to be operated at busy times.

The line climbs gently towards Vandyke Road, crossing a brook by the oddly named 'Swing-Swang Bridge' and then turns right to follow the road on a parallel course all the way to the terminus at Stonehenge Works. This is a classic stretch of industrial railway, sandwiched between the road and fields by hedges of hawthorn and blackberry. After a couple of tiny halts that mark temporary termini as the LBR gradually extended its operations, the vast Redland

Lafarge tile factory comes into view, a continuing link between the sand industry and the manufacture of building materials in the shape of brick and tile works.

Stonehenge Works takes its name from the Stonehenge Brickworks that once occupied the site. The railway's workshop buildings were built in 1918 by German prisoners-of-war and were formerly stables for the horses that hauled the skips around the quarries. The works is also used to illustrate the role of industrial railways at large, one exhibit being a Welsh slate quarry wagon loaded with slates. Plans are being developed to turn the works into a museum of the industrial railway, reflecting the importance of this collection of narrow gauge steam and diesel locomotives as the largest in the country.

They are a cosmopolitan lot, having worked in such places as Oman, Calcutta, Cameroon and Spain, as well as all over Britain. There are 10 steam locomotives, most owned by the LBR and a few on loan. The oldest and most curious is the vertical-boilered De Winton 0-4-0 named *Chaloner*, which once worked at slate quarries in North Wales. Her peculiar appearance has led to the nickname of 'coffee pot', though 'tea urn' would be equally apposite. The Baguley 0-4-0 tank *Rishra* spent its working life at the Pulta Pumping Station at Barrakpore near Calcutta, and was repatriated by the former head of ICI in India, Mike Satow, who was largely responsible for the creation of Delhi Railway Museum before he left the country. He found *Rishra* in semi-jungle with a washing-line tied to its chimney and had it restored as an exercise for engineering apprentices.

Under restoration is another extraordinary locomotive from India: Baldwin 4-6-0 tank No 778 worked on the steep railway that ran up to the hill station of Matheran, used by residents of Bombay to escape the heat.

The other engines represent the products of classic industrial locomotive builders such as Kerr Stuart in Stoke-on-Trent, Hunslet of Leeds, Orenstein & Koppel in Berlin and Andrew Barclay of Kilmarnock. The Kerr Stuart *Peter Pan* has the distinction of being the first steam locomotive to pass through the Channel

◀ **Elf** *was built in 1936 by Orenstein & Koppel of Drewitz near Berlin for the Likomba Banana Co. in Cameroon. It is fitted with a spark-arresting chimney for wood-burning, and is seen at Page's Park.*

Tunnel – not in steam, of course, but en route to a narrow gauge railway on the Continent (the relatively modest size of narrow gauge engines makes it easier for them to 'visit' other railways).

MID-HANTS RAILWAY

When the line that formed the Mid-Hants Railway was opened in 1865, Hampshire was not yet considered within commuting distance of London. Today Alton station is the terminus of electric commuter services from London Waterloo, but the character of the line that once ran on to Winchester is very much that of a cross-country branch line that could be called on to deputize as a main line when engineering works called for diversions.

In 1861 the Alton, Alresford & Winchester Railway, which soon changed its name to the Mid-Hants Railway, obtained powers for a 27-km (17-mile) line across cornfields and hop-growing downland along the Itchen Valley to Winchester. Apart from the expresses that periodically struggled up the line's steep gradients, and the local passenger service that survived until

➤ *Unrebuilt Bulleid Pacific No 34105* **Swanage** *climbs Medstead bank with an Alton–Alresford train. The Mid-Hants was often used as a diversionary route, making such scenes a common sight.*

1973, the main traffic was watercress from beds around Alresford. Until the coming of the railway, the growers' market was limited to the surrounding area because of the perishable nature of their product. Rail transport opened up profitable new markets and the industry flourished.

Proposals to take over the line and operate both diesel commuter and steam tourist trains were put forward as early as 1972 , when closure by British Rail was a near certainty. The ambitious plans to save the whole line as far as Winchester Junction faltered when the first share issue in early 1975 failed to meet its target. A second issue later that year, with the more modest goal of a steam service between Alton and Alresford, proved successful and allowed the purchase of the entire trackbed and a down payment on the track itself between Alresford and Ropley.

The line reopened between those stations on 30 April 1977, when the first train was hauled by N class 2-6-0 No 31874. Regrettably British Rail had lifted the track between Ropley and Alton – despite the obvious intention of reopening the section – so

☛ *In September 1955 London & South Western Railway M7 0-4-4 tank No 30479 pulls out of Alresford with the 11.12 Saturdays-only train to Alton.*

MID-HANTS RAILWAY

Length of line: *16km (10 miles)*
Operating periods:
Weekends March–end October;
many weekdays in school holidays.
Facilities:
Refreshments at stations and buffet on many trains;
shops, picnic area and viewing facilities at Ropley.
Access for disabled:
Toilets at Ropley and near Alresford station;
wheelchairs in brake compartment of all trains.
Public transport:
Rail to Alton: Stagecoach buses
(dial 100 for freefone County Bus Line).
Nearby tourist attractions:
Jane Austen's house, Hinton Ampner (NT),
Rotherfield Park, Northington Grange.
Address:
Alresford Station, Alresford,
Hampshire SO24 9JG.
Internet address: *http://www.itoeye.co.uk*
Telephone (information): *01962 733810*
Telephone (timetable): *01962 734866*

the Mid-Hants had to relay the line, relying on volunteer help. The first public train steamed into Medstead & Four Marks on 28 May 1983 and Alton was reached on 25 May 1985.

Few preserved railways enjoy such an easy connection with the main railway network: at Alton, Mid-Hants trains share an island platform with services operated by South West Trains to and from Waterloo. It is worth pausing to have a walk around Alton, and the Mid-Hants publishes a booklet with a suggested route. It takes in the Town Hall of 1813, in which the murderer of 'Sweet Fanny Adams' made his first appearance when it was in use as a court house. This still-current phrase has its origins in the gruesome fact that in 1867 Fanny Adams was murdered and cut into small pieces, at a time when Royal Navy sailors were beginning to receive meat of uncertain identity in tins...

Mid-Hants trains leave from platform 3 of Alton station and face a stiff climb at up to 1 in 60, passing a signal box on the right and entering a well-treed cutting that echoes the locomotive's exhaust beats.

◆ Close to the Mid-Hants Railway is the house at Chawton where Jane Austen lived from 1809 until 1817, writing here the final versions of her six novels.

About a mile south-west of Alton, the foundations of Butts Junction signal box can still be seen by the eagle-eyed. This controlled the trifurcation of the line, the right-hand branch turning north to Basingstoke and the left bearing south to Fareham and Portsmouth, while the Mid-Hants maintains its south-westerly course.

The Basingstoke branch was built as a light railway, opening as late as 1901, and never made a penny profit, closing as a wartime economy measure in 1917 and reopening for little more than a decade after it. As one of the few railways that closed before the Second World War, it attracted the attention of film companies looking for a railway set and featured in two classic films, *The Wrecker* (1929) and *Oh! Mr Porter* (1937) starring Will Hay, Moore Marriott and Graham Moffat.

As the line enters more open country with views

🔺 *This scene of Class M7 0-4-4T No 30053, normally resident on the Swanage Railway, posing as No 30479 at Medstead & Four Marks, shows how well many heritage lines have recreated the past.*

south over the downland, the village of Chawton comes into view. This was Jane Austen's home from 1809 to 1817, during which time she wrote the final versions of her six novels. A bracken-lined cutting and the soaring brickwork of Boyneswood bridge herald the approach to the first station, Medstead & Four Marks. With its attractive signal-box on the eastbound platform, this station has been delightfully restored in Southern Railway colours and upper quadrant signals of the period. Beside the well-tended flower-beds there is a topiary armchair.

There are extensive views to north and south across the rolling fields and woods as the line continues its south-westerly course to Ropley, where the railway's engine shed and workshops are located in new buildings on the south side of the line. As was often the case, the village that gave the station its name is 1.6km (1 mile) away, contributing to the decline of passenger revenue when bus services began after the First World War. The handsome brick station building on the westbound platform included residential accommodation for the station-master. The two platforms are connected by a footbridge that was rescued from North Tawton on the Exeter–Barnstaple line, and they are lit by lamps mounted on spiral-columned posts. Like Medstead & Four Marks, topiary is a feature of the station garden, with birds and chess pieces sculpted out of the shrubs. The station is a good place to watch the trains go by, for there is an attractive picnic site on the embankment above the eastbound platform.

The line drops steeply towards Alresford, allowing the fireman to relax as the train drifts downhill before passing through a deep chalk-lined cutting to arrive at the end of the line. A visitor centre is planned for the goods shed, but there is already plenty of interest in this pretty Georgian town to occupy an afternoon. Again, the Mid-Hants produces a booklet outlining a walk that takes in the town's most interesting buildings and some picturesque paths.

The town owes its appearance to two devastating fires within 50 years: the second, in 1736, destroyed so many houses built of thatch, wattle and daub that it was decreed that rebuilding should be in brick and tile. The heart of the town is Broad Street, just five minutes' walk from the station. At the end of Broad Street, past the old fire station, is the Globe, a fine 17th-century inn overlooking a nature reserve based on the 12-hectare (30-acre) Old Alresford Pond. The pub garden at the back has an enchanting view over the reed-fringed lake to wooded slopes beyond. The walk takes visitors past an idyllic thatched house that was once a fulling mill powered by the water from the pond. It also passes alongside the watercress beds that provided welcome traffic for the railway.

Today the railway is operated largely by an appropriate collection of Southern Railway locomotives or British Railways standard classes that are well suited to the demands of a steeply graded tourist railway. Unusually, only one of the former main line locomotives is a tank engine. The generously dimensioned footplates of most of the tender engines are put to good use on footplate experience courses.

One of the more unusual special events organized by the railway is the real ale train, which runs on designated weekends in conjunction with a number of regional real ale breweries. Passengers are able to compare a number of beers from casks carried in a gangwayed luggage van.

MOORS VALLEY RAILWAY

The Moors Valley Railway (MVR) is a 184mm (7¼in) gauge line with a difference. Most commercial miniature railways are quite simple in their layout and operation, with only one or two engines required to run the service. The MVR is operated like a busy main line in miniature, with full signalling from substantial signal boxes, and a large

overall roofed station at Kingsmere. Situated in a popular and attractive country park, five or six trains are required to cope with the large number of visitors. It opened in 1986 after moving from a site in nearby Christchurch. The layout of the long route was designed to be interesting for visitors, and even incorporates a spiral around an adventure playground.

The locomotive fleet has its origins in an innovative 0-4-2T built in 1968 by Roger Marsh. The concept was novel in that it enabled a driver – assuming he or she was of reasonably slender proportions – to sit in, rather than astride, the locomotive. Named *Tinkerbell*, it looked more like a narrow gauge engine than a miniature, and it spawned numerous successors, including the 13 locomotives that operate the MVR.

Apart from relieving the driver's back, the great advantage of these engines is that, by increasing their dimensions to accommodate the driver, more power can be extracted from a generous boiler and larger cylinders. This power is needed on the MVR, which was designed to carry 150,000 passengers a year, for which long trains are required. The gradients on the line are also taxing for a full train.

MOORS VALLEY RAILWAY

Length of line: *1.92km (1.2 miles)*
Operating periods:
  Every Sunday; Saturdays in March–October; daily in school holidays.
Facilities:
  Buffet, shop, adventure playground.
Access for disabled: *Special toilets.*
Public transport:
  Wilts & Dorset Bus X2 from Bournemouth/Ringwood to Ashley Heath.
Nearby tourist attractions:
  Dorset Heavy Horse Centre.
Address:
  Moors Valley Country Park, Horton Road, Ashley Heath, Nr Ringwood, Dorset BH24 2ET.
Telephone (information):
  01425 471415

▲Visitors to the Romney, Hythe & Dymchurch may well want to take a scenic detour at Hythe along the Royal Military Canal, which was built between 1804 and 1807.

ROMNEY, HYTHE & DYMCHURCH RAILWAY

The Romney, Hythe & Dymchurch Railway (RHDR) is a main line railway in miniature, with all the atmosphere of the real thing. It is double-track for most of its length, with one-third scale locomotives, signalling, licensed observation car and 11 steam locomotives, the majority of which are reworking of Sir Nigel Gresley's A1 Pacifics. The other unusual feature of the RHDR is that it has a much longer history than any line in this book except the Ravenglass & Eskdale Railway. Nearly all the standard gauge preserved railways are based on lines taken over from British Rail, but these two were set up as miniature gauge tourist attractions long before anyone had cause to think of saving the 'real thing'.

We have the prosperity of the real estate market in Melbourne, Victoria to thank for the RHDR. Rents from property worth over £1 million paid for one man's indulgence. The man was Captain J E P Howey, who had 'caught the 15-inch gauge bug' when he was invited by the well-known Northampton model-maker Bassett-Lowke to attend the opening of the Rhyl Miniature Railway in 1911.

For the next few years Howey vied with other enthusiasts to have the most powerful miniature locomotive, and built his first railway at Staughton Manor in Huntingdonshire. But the idea for something on the scale of the RHDR seems to have come from the man who would have been Howey's partner, had he not killed himself in the Italian Grand Prix at Monza in 1924. Count Louis Zborowski, who owned the real 'Chitty-Chitty-Bang-Bang' (a 23-litre Mercedes-Maybach), visited Bassett-Lowke's London shop at 112 Holborn shortly after the war in the company of Tsar Nicholas II's cousin and assassin of Rasputin. In conversation with an assistant of the firm, the two men talked about the idea of creating a miniature main line railway and all that goes with it.

Before he died, Zborowski ordered what became the RHDR's first two engines from Davey, Paxman of Colchester – but it was left to Howey to fulfil their

▶The outline of one of the RHDR's two locomotives based on the outline of a class of Canadian National Railway Pacifics contrasts with the Greenly-designed Pacific, which drew on Gresley's A1s.

ROMNEY, HYTHE & DYMCHURCH RAILWAY

Length of line: *21.6km (13½ miles)*

Operating periods:
Daily April–September; weekends in March and October.

Facilities:
Cafés at New Romney and Dungeness, shops, toy and model museum.

Access for disabled:
Wheelchair coach by arrangement; stairlift at New Romney to museum; special toilets at Hythe, Dymchurch and New Romney.

Public transport:
Bus from Folkestone station to Hythe.

Nearby tourist attractions:
Royal Military Canal, Dungeness Power Station Visitors' Centre, Lympne Castle.

Address:
New Romney Station, Kent TN28 8PL.

Internet address:
http://www.i-way.co.uk/~tburgess/rhdr.htm/rhdr

Telephone (information):
01797 362353/3633256

ambition for the railway itself. The idea for a line at Romney Marsh was suggested to Howey by the General Manager of the Southern Railway, Sir Herbert Walker, in August 1925. The public inquiry into the Light Railway Order was held within six months of Howey hearing the suggestion and construction was sufficiently far advanced for the Duke of York to ride on the footplate of No 2 *Northern Chief* with Howey in August 1926.

The 12.8-km (8-mile) railway was opened by the Lord Warden of the Cinque Ports on 16 July 1927. It immediately became a major tourist attraction, as well as a useful addition to the area's public transport – a school train is still operated, taking 200 children from the Dymchurch area to New Romney. Initially the line ran only from Hythe to New Romney, but the following year a 8.8-km (5½-mile) extension to Dungeness was opened, with a large return loop to reverse the trains.

During the Second World War the line became part of the home front when the area was taken over for military purposes and an armoured train was created using the 4-8-2 *Hercules*. The two armour-plated wagons on either side of the engine each sported a

➤No 2 Northern Chief is turned at Hythe, the northern terminus of the RHDR. No 2 was one of two engines ordered by Count Zborowski from Davey Paxman of Colchester.

pair of Lewis guns and a Boyes anti-tank rifle, later replaced by a Bofors gun. It was involved in a few incidents, one of which led to a claim of shooting down a Dornier. The RHDR also played a role in the construction of the pipeline that was to keep the invasion force supplied with fuel after D-Day, code-named PLUTO (Pipe Line Under The Ocean).

Pictures of the armoured train were published all over the world, and the publicity that was given to the railway's wartime role helped its popularity when peace returned. The section between Hythe and New Romney reopened in 1946 and people flocked to see the 'world's smallest public railway' in such numbers that the railway could barely cope with the crowds – a position exacerbated by a shortage of coaches, thanks to wartime neglect. In 1947 the publicity that attended a visit by Laurel and Hardy to reopen the Dungeness section only made matters worse.

The railway's prosperity continued through the 1950s, but as more people went abroad with the easing of currency restrictions, the railway went through a difficult period with two unsuccessful changes of owner. Finally a consortium under the then Hon W H McAlpine stepped in to save the railway from impending closure. Its fortunes have been turned round, and the physical condition of the railway has never been better – Howey left a legacy of much-needed remedial work to bring his parsimoniously

◄ No 8 **Hurricane** *waits to leave Hythe for New Romney. In common with No 7* **Typhoon,** **Hurricane** *was a three-cylinder locomotive with radial valve gear designed by Greenly.*

engineered bridges and buildings up to scratch.

Nobody could pretend that the route of the RHDR holds a candle to most tourist railways for scenery. Much of the inter-war development that abuts part of the line has done little for the area's appeal, but Romney Marsh has an individual character, enhanced by its associations with smuggling and skulduggery.

The line starts at the genteel seaside town of Hythe, where large hotels once hosted Saturday night black tie dinner-dances. This is the closest point for a walk along the Royal Military Canal, which was built between 1804 and 1807 as a line of defence against a possible invasion by Napoleon. Hythe is an imposing station with three platforms, an overall roof, signal box and turntable. The small engine shed is no longer used.

Once the houses of Hythe are left behind, there are open views across the marsh to the rise on which Lympne Castle stands. Parts of the castle date back to the 13th century. The first of many level-crossings is encountered at Burmarsh Road, now protected by automatic colour light signals. The first stop at Dymchurch gives an opportunity to see an example of Howey's economies when it came to buildings: the toilets are built into the step supports for the

footbridge. Few other original features of Howey's station remain.

Jefferstone Lane station is used by holidaymakers bound for the fine beach at St Mary's Bay. On the left you may see a long bungalow named 'The Long Boat', where Edith Nesbit, the author of *The Railway Children*, spent the last years of her life. She is buried at St Mary in the Marsh. The train is soon out into open country again, and after a gentle left-hand curve the line enters a rare cutting before diving into one of the two single bores that burrow under the main Folkestone to Hastings road.

New Romney station is the railway's headquarters, which have been extensively rebuilt and upgraded since Howey's times. The model railway that has long been an attraction has been developed into an attractively presented model exhibition, which is well worth a visit. The railway's single-line section begins at New Romney, with one passing loop on the way to Dungeness. The line leaves New Romney on top of what was once the sea wall, though tidal action has long ago silted up the former harbour.

Shingle is the dominant feature of the extension to Dungeness, and the rudimentary building materials of wood and asbestos used to build some of the houses give the area a distinctive, if hardly picturesque, character. The two lighthouses and two nuclear power stations mark the end of the line as the train describes the large return loop, pausing at Dungeness station. Here bird-watchers and horticulturists often detrain to admire the teeming bird life and the unusual plants that have found a home in this strange area.

The fleet of 11 steam locomotives and two diesels is maintained at the running shed and workshops at New Romney, where carriages are built as well as maintained. Of the seven Davey, Paxman engines, three are two-cylinder Pacifics, two are three-cylinder Pacifics and the final two are 4-8-2s built to haul ballast traffic that never developed as anticipated. Two Canadian-style Pacifics were built by the Yorkshire Engine Co. in 1931, and the original 0-4-0 contractors' engine built by Krauss of Munich has been repatriated and restored after languishing in a Belfast scrapyard.

◀No 2 **Northern Chief** *had the distinction of hauling the opening train, driven by the Duke of York with Gresley sitting on the tender, on 16 July 1927.*

SITTINGBOURNE & KEMSLEY LIGHT RAILWAY

Before Britain's politicians put their faith in roads and lorries to act as the principal arteries for the nation's commerce, there were thousands of private sidings and railways linking the national railway system with factories, warehouses, mines, quarries and ports. Now that saner councils prevail, some of these are being reinstated, but it is unlikely that any of them will be narrow gauge, like the Sittingbourne & Kemsley Light Railway (SKLR).

The first part of this remarkable preserved industrial railway was opened in 1906. Its purpose was to connect the Edward Lloyd & Co. paper-mill in Sittingbourne with a wharf on an inlet off the River Swale known as Milton Creek. This short section was soon extended when it became obvious that larger vessels and improved docking facilities would be required to cope with the increase in business. This expansion also resulted in a second mill being built halfway along the line at Kemsley Down.

Because both raw materials and finished products were brought in and taken out by sea, there was no need to worry about the interchange of wagons with the standard gauge railway network. Consequently Edward Lloyd was able to choose the minimum gauge that could handle the traffic, and 762mm (2ft 6in) was adopted.

The line worked round the clock when business demanded, and investment in new locomotives continued even after Bowater took over from Edward Lloyd in 1948. By the late 1950s, 13 locomotives were based on the railway, but in 1965 Bowater was advised that lorries would do the job better. Although the company accepted the recommendation, it did so with sufficient reluctance to offer the railway to the Locomotive Club of Great Britain (LCGB) in the hope that at least part of it would be saved.

Today the section from Sittingbourne to Kemsley Down is operated as a reminder of the characterful industrial railway that once kept thousands of lorry movements off Britain's roads. The journey is no scenic delight, passing for the first part through an area of light industry and the kind of scrubby, unkempt industrial hinterland that is often found around backwaters. Poorly-drained fields and the odd orchard improve the surroundings on the way to the mill compound that

forms the terminus of the line at Kemsley Down, where the locomotive depot is situated.

A fleet of seven steam engines is based there, including two of the original locomotives, *Premier* and *Leader*, which were both built in 1905 by that prolific builder of industrial locomotives, Kerr Stuart, at its California Works in Stoke-on-Trent. Both are 0-4-2 tanks, but by the early 1920s more powerful engines were needed. The first 0-6-2T was again built by Kerr Stuart, but for subsequent engines Edward Lloyd turned to W G Bagnall of Stafford. They produced four more 0-6-2Ts and three of them are still to be seen on the SKLR: *Alpha* (1932), *Triumph* (1934) and *Superb* (1940). Other engines include a later Kerr Stuart 0-4-2T *Melior* and a Bagnall fireless locomotive – so-called because it had no independent means of generating steam. These locomotives filled their boilers with steam from a central supply generated by a stationary boiler attached to the works.

There is unfortunately no access to Kemsley Down except by rail, so all visitors have to join the trains at Sittingbourne.

◆Kerr Stuart 0-4-2 saddle tank **Melior** *of 1924 amid typical terrain of this industrial part of Kent. The SKLR is a rare survivor of a narrow gauge line linking shipping operations and factory.*

SITTINGBOURNE & KEMSLEY LIGHT RAILWAY

Length of line: *3.2km (2 miles)*
Operating periods:
  Sundays in April–mid-October; Bank Holidays.
Facilities:
  Shop, refreshments, picnic area, museum and depot at Kemsley Down.
Public transport: *Sittingbourne station.*
Nearby tourist attractions:
  Dolphin Yard Sailing Barge Museum.
Address: *Access from Milon Road.*
Telephone (information): *01634 852672*
Telephone (timetable): *01795 424899*

SPA VALLEY RAILWAY

The south-east of England was once well served by a comprehensive network of cross-country lines that linked the market towns and villages of the fertile counties of Kent and Sussex. Today, there is little to recall many of these lines but an overgrown cutting or a station converted into a home, leaving a railway network that focuses on London and commuter services.

One of those meandering byways survives in the few miles of the Spa Valley Railway (SVR), though the railway directors who authorized its construction in 1862 would have been upset to have it so described. The magnificent station at Tunbridge Wells West, adjacent to the SVR but now converted into a family restaurant, is evidence of their hopes for the town's second route to London. Its sheer size, decorative clock-tower and polychromatic brickwork may seem

➤ *The Pantiles, though now largely given over to shops, wine bars and restaurants, were once the centre of activity when Tunbridge Wells was a fashionable 18th-century spa town.*

ostentatious for a secondary route, but in 1912 there were 115 train movements a day at the station. Even in 1956 there were 70 passenger and 5 goods trains a day.

The SVR's largest building is the original locomotive shed that provided the motive power for many of these trains. It is not only an extremely valuable resource for the railway, but is also probably the finest surviving locomotive shed after the London & Birmingham Railway roundhouse in Camden, which is in a class of its own. The SVR had to re-roof the four-road shed but it retains its cast-iron round-headed windows and, above all, the atmosphere of those Meccas of steam for generations of enthusiasts.

The enthusiasts who set up a society to preserve the line, and acquired it in 1996 after years of hard work, at least did not have to relay the track. Although the line was closed by British Rail in July 1985, the track was not precipitately ripped up as of old, when no one in power had the foresight to see that some closed railways might one day be needed again. Finding locomotives and carriages with which to run

the trains has not been so easy: as a late arrival on the railway preservation scene, the SVR could not look to British Rail as a source of historic items. So its locomotives and rolling stock are derived mostly from other preserved railways or failed schemes.

The journey over this former London Brighton & South Coast Railway line begins at a new platform built opposite the engine shed. The old platforms were swept away to build a car-park and approach road for the nearby Sainsbury's. The new station is on the western outskirts of the town, so soon after a departing blast on the whistle, you are leaving the last houses behind and moving into countryside.

A mile or so of thick woods on the left and more open country on the right brings passengers to High Rocks Halt for the eponymous pub and restaurant. There was once a rudimentary halt here, with a rickety

➤ *This area is now a car-park, but Tunbridge Wells West station building survives. Bulleid Pacific No 34066* **Spitfire** *hauls an enthusiasts' special, with Q1 0-6-0 No 33027 on the right.*

◆ *The London Brighton & South Coast Railway engine shed at Tunbridge Wells West, one of the finest in preservation, is now the workshop and shed of the Spa Valley.*

SPA VALLEY RAILWAY

Length of line: *4.8km (3 miles)*

Operating periods:

Weekends mid-March–end October;
some weekdays in school holidays.

Facilities:

Souvenir shop, light refreshments, depot open.

Access for disabled: *Phone before visit.*

Public transport:

Buses from Tunbridge Wells station to Sainsbury's
(adjacent to West station).

Nearby tourist attractions:

The Pantiles, Groombridge Place.

Address:

West Station, Tunbridge Wells,
Kent TN4 8HL.

Internet address:

http://www.uel.ac.uk/pers/1278/rly-pres/spa.html

Telephone (information): *01892 537715*

staircase down to the wooden platform, but it closed in 1952. Today's halt is graced with fluted lamp standards and ornamental lamps and offers a safe way to reach, and more particularly leave, the virginia creeper-covered pub.

The line then passes converted oast houses seen across acres of sunflowers, birch woods with bracken undergrowth and fields of horses. As you approach Groombridge station, the parkland of Groombridge Place can be seen across the valley. It is only a pleasant 0.8-km (½-mile) walk from the station to the moated 17th-century house and its splendid gardens (reduced admission for SVR passengers).

The handsome old station at Groombridge is in use as offices, so the SVR is building a successor on a new platform to the west of the old. Beyond Groombridge, the line divided into three: the northern arm headed for London via Ashurst and Hever; the western branch went to East Grinstead and Three Bridges (now the Forest Way Walk); and the southern branch went to Eridge, where the line again divided for Lewes and Eastbourne. It is hoped that in the next century, the SVR will be reopened to Eridge. This would provide a public transport link to the northern end of the Cuckoo Trail path for walkers and cyclists that extends to Eastbourne.

CHAPTER 2
THE WEST COUNTRY

During the 20th century, the West Country came to be strongly associated with holidays beside the sea, bringing a welcome influx of passengers to the characterful branch lines that served so many of the resorts. Several of these lines have been preserved and now perform a valued role as public transport as well as being a source of entertainment.

◀ *The East Somerset Railway has kept its Great Western character. Here GWR 0-4-2 tank No 1450 passes the magnificent GWR-style engine shed built at Cranmore.*

▲ *Within sight of the Gloucestershire Warwickshire Railway and once served by a halt on the line are the remains of the Cistercian Hailes Abbey, founded in 1246.*

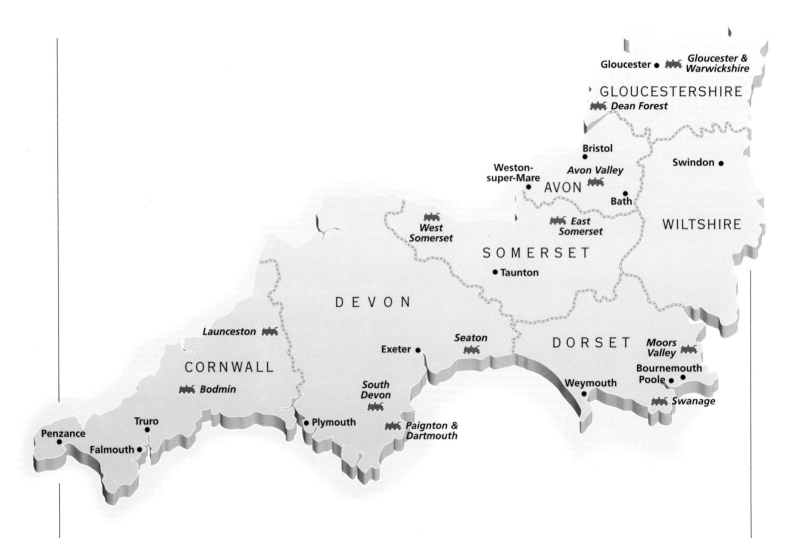

Gloucester • 🚂 *Gloucester & Warwickshire*

GLOUCESTERSHIRE

🚂 *Dean Forest*

Bristol •

Weston-super-Mare • *Avon Valley*

AVON 🚂

Swindon •

Bath •

🚂 *East Somerset*

WILTSHIRE

🚂 *West Somerset*

SOMERSET

• Taunton

DEVON

Launceston • 🚂

Seaton 🚂

Exeter •

DORSET

🚂 *Moors Valley*

CORNWALL

🚂 *Bodmin*

South Devon 🚂

Bournemouth • Poole •

Weymouth •

🚂 *Swanage*

Truro •

Plymouth •

🚂 *Paignton & Dartmouth*

Penzance •

Falmouth •

AVON VALLEY RAILWAY

The Midland Railway opened its line from the triangular junction at Mangotsfield to Bath in 1869, enabling it to undertake a joint lease of the impecunious Somerset & Dorset Railway on to Bournemouth six years later. Once an important double-track line, it closed in 1966.

Initially named the Bristol Suburban Railway, the Avon Valley Railway (AVR) has reopened a 3.2-km (2-mile) stretch of the line between Mangotsfield and Bath, based at Bitton station. It shares the trackbed with the now-famous Bristol & Bath cycle path, which was the first project of Sustrans, currently building the National Cycle Network.

Trains run to a new northern terminus at Oldland Common, which can accommodate five-coach trains. Besides a collection of industrial engines, the AVR has two London Midland & Scottish Railway locomotives and one Southern Railway Bulleid Pacific.

AVON VALLEY RAILWAY

Length of line: *3.2km (2 miles)*
Operating periods:
  Please contact for operating dates.
Facilities: *Buffet.*
Access for disabled:
  Coach converted to accommodate wheelchairs.
Public transport:
  Badgerline No 332 between Bristol and Bath.
Nearby tourist attractions: *Beckford Tower.*
Address:
  Bitton Station, Willsbridge,
  Bristol BS15 6ED.
Telephone (information):
  0117 329 5538 (weekends)
Telephone (timetable):
  0117 329 7296

BODMIN & WENFORD RAILWAY

The branch lines of the Great Western Railway (GWR) in the West Country had a distinctive character that endeared them to generations of holiday-makers and railway enthusiasts alike. Small-wheeled prairie (2-6-2) tanks hustled detached portions or slip coaches off main line expresses along the final miles to seaside resorts. The flower-filled stations were marked by the distinctive Scots pines that so often clustered around GWR stations, and exuded the combined smells of Welsh coal, hot oil, steam and seaborne ozone.

Cornwall's only steam-worked standard gauge railway is the Bodmin & Wenford Railway (BWR), reopened in 1990 between Bodmin and the junction with British Rail (BR) at Bodmin Parkway. In typical GWR fashion, Bodmin Parkway used to be called Bodmin Road, and the line between there and the county town first opened in 1887. The link with the

On loan from the Birmingham Railway Museum, GWR 0-6-0 pannier tank No 7760 double heads a train at Bitton with GNR J52 0-6-0 saddle tank No 68846. Extensions to the line are planned.

line of the London & South Western Railway (LSWR) between its own station in Bodmin (known as North) and Wadebridge opened the following year. Sand, fish and china clay became the principal freight traffic. Passenger traffic during the Second World War soared with numerous troop trains to Bodmin General (another typical GWR name) for the adjacent barracks of the Duke of Cornwall's Light Infantry. In 1944 Field Marshall Montgomery and General Eisenhower arrived at Bodmin by train for a visit to the regiment.

Passenger traffic ceased in January 1967, but freight lingered on until 1983. In the meantime, Bodmin General had been the subject of an unsuccessful attempt by the Great Western Society to preserve the

BODMIN & WENFORD RAILWAY

Length of line: *5.6km (3½ miles) Bodmin Parkway–Bodmin; 4km (2½ miles) Bodmin–Boscarne.*

Operating periods:
Daily mid-April and June–September; Saturdays and/or Sundays in April, October and December.

Facilities: *Buffet, shop.*

Access for disabled: *Please telephone before visit.*

Public transport:
Cross-platform change with Wales & West trains at Bodmin Parkway. Through tickets from stations in Devon and Cornwall.

Nearby tourist attractions:
Lanhydrock (NT), Restormel Castle (EH), Bodmin Farm Park, Light Infantry Museum, Fitzgerald Lighting Factory Tours.

Address:
Bodmin General Station, Bodmin, Cornwall PL31 1AQ.

Telephone (information): *01208 73666*

⬥ *The china clay workings on the Wenford Bridge branch were the last haunt of Beattie 2-4-0 well tanks, like No 30587 seen here at Dunmere Siding in August 1953.*

terminus; they quit the station in 1977, leaving the field open for a fresh initiative in 1984 that became the BWR. Thanks to considerable help from North Cornwall District Council, the line was secured and renovation work began.

The BWR had the distinction of becoming the first preserved railway over which regular commercial freight services were operated, taking vans of light fittings from the siding of Fitzgerald Lighting at Bodmin and handing them over to BR at Parkway for onward movement to distribution centres in England and Scotland. Although this ceased in late 1992, it was revived in 1996 by the new freight operator, English Welsh & Scottish Railway. In the same year the BWR extended its operations by reopening the former line to Boscarne Junction to a new station at Boscarne. This may become part of a revival of the freight only line that once served the china clay dries at Wenford; this would relieve the narrow country roads of 8,510 lorry journeys a year and help to increase still further the BWR's freight revenue.

Arriving at wooded Bodmin Parkway, there is a cross-platform change to reach the BWR which shares the eastbound island platform with main line trains. The beautiful National Trust house of Lanhydrock, largely 19th-century but looking much older, is reached by a pretty 2.8-km (1¾-mile) path from the station. The BWR curves sharply away from the main line, across the five-arch Bodmin Road Viaduct and on to a fierce 1 in 40 bank, which tests the skill of both driver and fireman, who has the handicap of the wait at Parkway, allowing enough time for clinker to start forming in the firebox.

With regulator wide open and a thunderous exhaust, the locomotive battles up the bank between a row of ancient poplars and under the A38 to

Colesloggett Halt, where many break the journey to enjoy the walks and cycle trails through Cardinham Woods. A yellow-arrowed footpath links the station and the woods, in which a café and cycle hire may be found. The BWR's informative guide book suggests various walks from the halt, and from its other stations.

The halt is still on a stiff gradient, so descending passengers can watch the locomotive struggle to get the train on the move again. Three bridges carry the A30 and A38 over the railway, and there are views to the left over Bodmin Moor as the gradient eases to a

➥ *A freight train hauled by 0-6-0 pannier tank No 1369, which was introduced in 1934, is seen here making its way from Boscarne Junction to Bodmin General.*

A drive leads from Bodmin Parkway station to the National Trust house at Lanhydrock. The delightful gatehouse was built in 1636–51, probably as a banqueting room for ladies.

'mere' 1 in 61. On the outskirts of Bodmin, the sidings of Fitzgerald Lighting can be seen on the right, where one of the BWR's largest locomotives, Southern Railway West Country class Pacific No 34007 *Wadebridge*, is being restored to working order.

As the train passes under a bridge at the throat of Bodmin station, the Boscarne line curves sharply to the west, followed on the left by the site of the single-road engine shed that closed in 1962. Its ash pit is still used for raking out the fire and ashpan. The conical water tower that once stood here now fills the tanks of locomotives at the Great Western Society's Didcot Railway Centre. The current engine shed is passed on the right as the train draws to a halt at the attractive stone-built station.

The section on to Boscarne is so sharply curved in places that check rails are needed – a second inside rail that guides the flanges and prevents any tendency to 'riding up'. It is also as steeply graded as the section from Bodmin Parkway, so stirring noises from the front are guaranteed. The line offers fine moorland views to the south, and of the monument to General Gilbert, who counted Sir Walter Ralegh among his ancestors. The train draws to a halt at a platform built on the trackbed of the Bodmin & Wadebridge Railway, which opened as early as 1834.

In due course, the BWR will have an appropriate locomotive for its history as a GWR branch line: 2-6-2T No 5552 was based at Newton Abbot and Truro sheds before being sent to Barry scrapyard in South Wales, and sister engines worked over the Bodmin branch between the 1930s and 1960s. It was saved from the blowtorch in 1986 and is being gradually restored. Besides a GWR heavy freight engine, 2-8-0 No 3802, the BWR has a variety of former industrial tank engines and some main line diesels. Its most historic coach is a 1910 GWR toplight corridor third, but its restoration will be a major challenge. Appropriately the railway has a number of the distinctive 'hooded' china clay wagons that were such a common sight on the line for many decades.

GWR 0-6-0 pannier tank No 7714 on a photographers' special freight working. The 1930-built locomotive normally resides on the Severn Valley Railway.

DEAN FOREST RAILWAY

The antecedents of the Dean Forest Railway (DFR) make it one of the select group of heritage railways that date from the era of horse-drawn tramways. Opened in 1810 and built by the Severn & Wye Railway (SWR), it furthered the extraction of the Forest of Dean's mineral resources that had been begun by the Romans. By 1868 the line

DEAN FOREST RAILWAY

Length of line: *3.2km (2 miles)*
Operating periods:
Sundays April–September;
Wednesdays in June and July; Tuesdays, Wednesdays, Thursdays and Saturdays in August.
Facilities: *Buffet, shop, museum.*
Access for disabled: *Access to facilities and trains.*
Public transport: *Lydney main line station.*
Nearby tourist attractions:
Clearwell Caves & Iron Mines,
Dean Heritage Centre (Soudley).
Address:
Forest Road, Lydney,
Gloucestershire GL15 4ET.
Telephone (information): *01594 845840*
Telephone (timetable): *01594 843423*

had been fully upgraded to steam-operated standard gauge railway standards, with passenger as well as goods services. In 1894 the SWR was jointly purchased by the Great Western (GWR) and Midland railways. However, the railway between Lydney Town and Lydbrook Junction became one of the very first railways in Britain to have its passenger services withdrawn, as early as July 1929.

☛ *The industrial function of most pre-preservation trains in the Forest of Dean has proved irresistible to many photographers. Here small-wheeled prairie No 5541 is seen at Middle Forge, with a freight for photographers.*

Freight services continued until 1976, when the British Rail-operated stone trains from Marsh sidings to the junction with the Newport–Gloucester main line at Lydney ceased running. Four years later BR offered the branch for sale. The DFR had been formed in 1970 in response to rumours about the branch line's closure, and finally it was able to start negotiations to buy it. The process took five years, but in 1985 the DFR secured its purchase. With the nucleus of its locomotive and rolling stock collection, the DFR had originally occupied the goods shed and adjacent siding at Parkend, but in 1974 it took the courageous step of moving to Norchard, where there

was more land for its headquarters and fewer restrictions for its operations.

The site at Norchard has been created out of an overgrown clearing in the forest, once the site of a colliery that employed 400 men but which closed in 1957. The DFR site is on two levels: the running lines and station on the west side are at a higher level, while the DFR's yard and sidings on the east side are at a lower level. The largest building is a three-track restoration shed and workshop that came from Newport Docks. The booking office building is from Yatton on the Bristol–Taunton line. The attractive signal box at the end of platform 3 is typical of the all-wood GWR type of box and came from Mileage Yard at Gloucester.

Services currently operate through the thickly wooded valley between Lydney Junction and Norchard, calling at St Mary's Halt for the adjacent large boating lake and wildfowl haven. The cast-iron footbridge here dates from 1892 and must be one of the very few such structures to be listed. The last

➡️*Pannier tank No 9681, seen in the thick of the forest, was the 75th locomotive to be rescued from Barry scrapyard. The engine had spent most of its career in Wales, based at Tondu and Oswestry.*

0.38km (¼ mile) brings the railway to the terminus at Lydney Junction, where a recent addition is the flat-roofed signal box that once stood at Heysham in Lancashire.

The DFR is being extended north to Parkend, work beginning in February 1996 to prepare the line between Whitecroft and Parkend for complete relaying of the track. This has been completed and a large amount of work has been done to the station site at Parkend, including the construction of a four-coach platform and run-round loop. The wooden station buildings were removed as long ago as 1929, following withdrawal of passenger services, so they have to be rebuilt. The signal box from Walnut Tree Junction at Taffs Well in South Wales is being re-erected to control operations at Parkend.

The DFR locomotives are all tank engines, mostly of industrial origin but including a GWR pannier tank and a small-wheeled 2-6-2. The most historic engine is Taff Vale Railway 0-6-2 tank No 28, built at West Yard Locomotive Works in Cardiff in 1897. Typical of hundreds of medium sized tank engines that dragged an endless series of coal trains through the valleys of South Wales, the engine is on loan from the National Railway Museum and is being restored to working order.

◀ *The unremunerative nature of many of the short freight trains that threaded the Forest of Dean during the last days of British Railways' operations can be deduced from this view of pannier No 2025 at Lydney.*

EAST SOMERSET RAILWAY

Nearly all Britain's heritage railways have been the result of a shared vision by a number of people with diverse skills. Unusually, the East Somerset Railway (ESR) was the idea of one man, and he attributes its creation to the African elephant. In 1967 David Shepherd returned from New York, where every painting in his one-man exhibition of African wildlife had been sold. On the strength of that success, he telephoned British Rail and bought two steam locomotives.

The ESR came into being after a long search for a permanent home for them, which included an attempt to save the Longmoor Military Railway in Hampshire. The transformation of the derelict site at Cranmore on the Great Western Railway (GWR) Witham–Wells–Yatton branch, which David Shepherd bought in 1972, has been achieved by the usual teamwork that underpins every preserved railway. Only the boarded-up station building, the only original remaining station on the entire branch, and the signal box survived. Both have been restored, and the signal box became an art gallery of natural history and railway subjects until the need for more space compelled its transfer to a new

---

EAST SOMERSET RAILWAY

Length of line: *4.4km (2¾ miles)*
Operating periods:
Daily in July–August; Wednesdays to Sundays in June and September; Saturdays and Sundays in April, May and October, Bank Holidays.
Facilities:
Restaurant, shop, art gallery, museum, engine shed, children's play area.
Access for disabled: *Easy access to facilities.*
Address:
Cranmore Railway Station, Shepton Mallet, Somerset BA4 4QP.
Telephone (information): *01749 880417*

building on the station. This has been created by dismantling and re-erecting stone by stone buildings from Wells and Lodge Hill, which have been added to the new, though period-style, station house built in 1973.

The most impressive building at Cranmore is the GWR-style, brick-built engine shed and workshop, built from scratch on the site of a Marcroft wagon repair depot and formally opened by Prince Bernhard of the Netherlands in 1975. This houses the engines bought by David Shepherd and some of the other locomotives that are based at the ESR.

The line was originally opened as the East Somerset Railway in 1858. It was built to broad gauge (2140mm/7ft 0¼in) and operated by the GWR, which bought out the ESR in 1874 prior to conversion to standard gauge in the same year. Cranmore was once a busy station thanks to the stone traffic that was transferred here from a tramway that linked Waterlip Quarry and the railway sidings to the north west of the station. A measure of the importance of this traffic was that the four stone-traffic sidings handled up to 100 wagons a day at the peak of the traffic. Milk and strawberries also provided an important source of revenue on the branch. Passenger traffic ceased in 1963 and most freight the following year, but the connection with the main railway network has remained intact, thanks to the survival of bitumen traffic between Essex and Cranmore until 1985 and subsequently to the vast quarries of Foster Yeoman and ARC at Merehead.

➤*No Great Northern Railway J52 saddle tank ever worked the East Somerset Railway, but No 1247, built at Doncaster in 1899, looks striking in the countryside around Cranmore.*

The Great Western branch lines of the West Country had a tremendous appeal, largely because of the delightful scenery through which they passed. Milk trains were a common sight, like this one at Cranmore.

Although the journey is quite short, some steep gradients up to the summit at Merryfield Lane give an opportunity for the engines to exert themselves. Leaving Cranmore station, the train passes on the right the sidings and engine shed. Just beyond is the halt of Cranmore West for passengers wishing to visit the engine shed, viewing platform in the workshop and picnic site. Moving into open country, two ancient burial mounds can be seen to the right before the train slows for the halt at Merryfield Lane. The terminus of operations until the track was relaid further west, the halt is now used by picnickers. Nearby is a siding close to Doulting stoneworks: the quarry that served it is extremely old, having produced the stone for Wells Cathedral. The railway developed a traffic in large blocks of freestone until Doulting siding closed in about 1948.

The train now descends at 1 in 56 and passes through the limestone Doulting cutting, which not only produced the stone for bridges at Cranmore and Shepton Mallet in the 1850s but is now of such interest on account of its fossils that it is designated a Site of Special Scientific Interest. Fine views over this lovely part of Somerset accompany a gentle right-hand curve that brings the train to the terminus at Mendip Vale, where a five-coach platform was completed by volunteers in 1993. The engine runs round the train and the fire is prepared for the stiff climb back up to Merryfield Lane.

David Shepherd's two original purchases – the huge 9F 2-10-0 No 92203 *Black Prince* for heavy freight and Class 4MT 4-6-0 No 75029 *The Green Knight* (both names given since preservation) – have been joined by various tank engines, notably London Brighton & South Coast Railway Class E1 No B110, built at Brighton in 1877.

GLOUCESTERSHIRE WARWICKSHIRE RAILWAY

Very few major railways were built after the beginning of the 20th century, but the Great Western Railway (GWR) line that linked Birmingham with Cheltenham via Stratford and Honeybourne was

The atmosphere of the steam railway at night, with steam swirling around gas- and oil-lit lamps, has made night photography sessions particularly popular. GWR 0-4-2 tank No 1450 is here seen at Toddington.

an exception. It was built to main line standards, with double track and bridges strong enough for all but the heaviest locomotives. The section between Cheltenham and Honeybourne opened in 1904–5. It became the route of Birmingham–Cardiff expresses, operated later by diesel railcars with buffet facilities, and the 'Cornishman' between Wolverhampton and Penzance. It was also a useful freight route – it was freight traffic that kept this section open until 1977 following the withdrawal of passenger services in March 1968.

Some of those who had campaigned to keep the line open now sought to reopen it, forming the

Gloucestershire Warwickshire Railway (GWRly) to buy the line from Stratford to Cheltenham. This proved too ambitious, but in 1981 the still-extensive 25.6-km (16-mile) section between Cheltenham and the picturesque Cotswold town of Broadway was purchased. Dismantling of the line had taken place in 1979, making the task of the GWRly much harder.

Starting at the intermediate station of Toddington, work began to relay the line southwards, the first public services beginning in April 1984. The line has been progressively extended and now reaches the site of the station at Gotherington, which awaits reconstruction. Apart from finding second-hand track from a variety of sources, this has entailed the rebuilding of Winchcombe station and work to ensure the structural integrity of the bridges and tunnel.

Toddington station building was still standing when the GWRly took over the line, but the platforms had

GLOUCESTERSHIRE WARWICKSHIRE RAILWAY

Length of line: *10.4km (6½ miles)*
Operating periods:
Sundays throughout the year; some summer weekdays.
Facilities: *Buffet, shop, narrow gauge railway.*
Access for disabled: *None.*
Nearby tourist attractions:
Hailes Abbey (NT/EH), Stanway House, Winchcombe – Folk, Police and Railway museums.
Address:
The Station, Toddington, Cheltenham, Gloucestershire GL54 5DT.
Telephone (information): *01242 621405*

been removed when the line closed to passengers. Thousands of engineering blues (bricks) had to be found and cleaned to rebuild the platform faces, and paving slabs were recovered from Gloucester, Cheltenham and Birmingham Snow Hill to edge the platforms. The shell of the signal box also survived, but the lever frame had to be imported from Earlswood Lakes on the outskirts of Birmingham.

As trains leave Toddington they pass on the right the former goods shed, which survived to become part of the GWRly's locomotive maintenance facilities. Running parallel with the standard gauge is the 610mm (2ft) gauge passenger-carrying North

☛*British Railways-built Castle class 4-6-0 No 7029* **Clun Castle**, *on loan from Birmingham Railway Museum, heads west out of Winchcombe station. The line is planned to reach Cheltenham.*

▲On loan Jubilee three-cylinder 4-6-0 No 45596 Bahamas *near Hailes Abbey with a rake of maroon British Railways Mark I coaches, recalling the last workings of Stanier's popular class on the Settle & Carlisle line.*

Gloucestershire Railway, on which a wonderful variety of British- and German-built engines can be seen, some brought to England after service in such places as Poland and Natal. A delightful Midland Railway (MR) signal box dating from 1920 and recovered from California Crossing in Gloucester controls the fine array of GWR and MR signals.

To the left is the long limestone escarpment of the Cotswold Hills overlooking the Vale of Evesham, through which the GWRly runs. The produce of the fruit trees through the Vale was a major source of goods revenue for the railway and accounted for the size of the goods yard at stations serving lightly populated villages such as Toddington. Just to the east is the village of Didbrook, which boasts a 15th-century cruck cottage. Residents of the village had a path to the now-vanished halt of Hailes Abbey, built by the GWR to allow passengers to visit the Cistercian abbey founded in 1246; the extensive ruins are owned by the National Trust but looked after by English Heritage.

Remains of medieval strip farming are followed by farming of indirect benefit to the railway: a herd of goats owned by a GWRly society member and bred for their Angora wool (for mohair) may be seen grazing the railway embankments; naturally this saves having to cut back the vegetation. As the line swings to the west, the kiln of Winchcombe Pottery may be seen to the north of the line before the train draws into the station that lies to the north of the pretty market town.

The station here had to be completely rebuilt, because only the goods shed and weighbridge survived. Each building has been sited as close as possible to the originals. The attractive main building came from Monmouth (Troy) and is of rather incongruous Monmouthshire sandstone. The up platform building is from Clifford in Gwent and the signal box is from Hall Green in Birmingham. The goods shed serves as the carriage and wagon workshop.

Soon after leaving Winchcombe, a deepening cutting heralds Greet Tunnel, at 633m (693yd) the second longest on a preserved railway. Daylight cannot be seen through it because it is built on a gentle curve. The area around the western portal was the site of one of the camps set up to house the navvies who built the railway.

➤Small-wheeled GWR prairie tank No 5531 takes water at Launceston in 1958, six years after trains from Plymouth started using the Southern Region station in the town.

As the train nears the current terminus at Gotherington, there are splendid views of the Vale of Evesham and the Malvern Hills to the north-west.

The GWRly's intention is to complete reconstruction of the railway south to Cheltenham Racecourse station before turning to the northern section towards Broadway, which includes the 15-arch Toddington Viaduct, one of the main structures on the line.

Most of the main line locomotives based on the GWRly are being restored, so it relies on visiting engines for some of its traction requirements, though several of its industrial locomotives are serviceable.

LAUNCESTON STEAM RAILWAY

The Launceston Steam Railway (LSR) begins at a station located in the town's Newport Industrial Estate. Standing on the platform at Launceston today, it is hard to believe that this was once a hive of railway

activity. The estate is built on the site of the town's two adjacent stations: a terminus served by the Great Western Railway (GWR) branch line from Plymouth and a through station on the London & South Western Railway's (LSWR) long line from Exeter to Padstow. Each had its own goods shed, engine shed and turntable, though from 1952 the Plymouth trains ran into the Southern Region station over a spur put in during the Second World War. Besides the town's passengers and the nine- or ten-coach summer excursion trains, freight traffic was substantial: in 1957, for example, 750 containers of fresh meat and 625 cattle trucks were loaded here.

In a pattern repeated all over Britain, the lines were rapidly and deliberately run down during the 1960s,

➥ The various exhibitions in the buildings around Launceston station are an added attraction. With a walk along the river and visit to the farm at the far end, it is easy to spend a day here.

LAUNCESTON STEAM RAILWAY

Length of line: *4km (2½ miles)*
Operating periods:
Daily except Saturdays and Spring Bank Holiday until end September; Sundays and Tuesdays from Easter to SBH and in October.
Facilities: *Buffet, shop, museum.*
Access for disabled:
Easy access except to bookshop.
Nearby tourist attractions:
Launceston Castle, Lawrence House Museum.
Address:
'Steam Railway', Launceston,
Cornwall PL15 8DA.
Telephone (information): *01566 775665*

the Plymouth line closing in 1962 and the Padstow line in 1966. Five years later an engineer named Nigel Bowman approached Launceston Council about the possibility of building a 600mm (1ft 11⅜in) gauge railway along the trackbed to the west of the town. Their encouraging response led to the opening of the first section from the town's former gasworks siding, just west of the Southern station, in 1983. Gradual extensions along the Kensey Valley have brought the railway to Newmills.

The ESR begins amid an eclectic group of buildings. The workshops and museum are housed in the attractive former Launceston Gas Company buildings that were once threatened with demolition for 13 houses. The booking office and cafeteria occupy what was once a three-bedroomed bungalow built by Boulton & Paul and sold at the first Ideal Home Exhibition in 1919. The station canopy from Tavistock North was a gift from West Devon District Council.

Leaving the station, the train curves behind some houses and passes underneath a stone and iron aqueduct built by the railway as a leat for Town Mills. The River Kensey is crossed by a two-arch bridge. Hunts Crossing has a passing loop and halt for passengers wishing to picnic by the river, courtesy of the local farmer. Broader views over the surrounding countryside may be enjoyed on the second half of the journey through the request stop at Canna Park to the terminus at Newmills.

A leaflet is available describing the walks from Newmills, and there is a riverside farm park and watermill close by, offering various indoor and outdoor games for children. On the return to Launceston, there is the museum of stationary steam engines, railway memorabilia, vintage cars and motor cycles in the gasworks building. A leaflet describes a town walk, taking in the nearby priory ruins and the medieval Priors Bridge.

The locomotives that operate the LSR are a delight: the four steam locomotives once worked in the slate quarries of North Wales and were built by the Hunslet Engine Company in Leeds or WG Bagnall in Stafford. The youngest was built in 1906, the oldest in

➤ *The scene at Launceston following the arrival of 5567 with the mid-morning train from Plymouth North Road, 20 December 1955. Another 4575 Class 2–6–2T is at the other end preparing to return on the next service to Plymouth.*

☛Coleton Fishacre is within easy reach of the Paignton & Dartmouth. Now cared for by the National Trust, the house was built in the late 1920s for the D'Oyly Carte family and has lovely gardens.

1883. The coaches, although newly built, are of interest for the origins of their design: two are based on Manx Electric Railway cars with toast-rack seating and one is a replica of a carriage on the curious Torrington & Marland Railway in North Devon.

PAIGNTON & DARTMOUTH STEAM RAILWAY

One of the busiest of the Great Western Railway's (GWR) holiday lines in the West Country was the 22-km (13¾-mile) branch from Aller Junction south of Newton Abbot to Kingswear. It was really not a branch line at all: from Aller to Goodrington Sands it was double track, built to take the heaviest locomotives, even the King class. It was the destination of named trains and even, for a while, a Pullman train. Moreover its engineer, until his death in 1859, was the great Isambard Kingdom Brunel.

The first section, 6.4km (4 miles) from Aller to a station for Torquay that was later to be called Torre, was opened in December 1848. It was another 11 years before the line was extended for a further 4.8km (3 miles) to Paignton. A measure of the civil engineering works required is that this section entailed 20 bridges, a viaduct and a tunnel (removed when the line was doubled in 1908–10). The next 4.8km (3 miles) to a temporary station at Oldway near Churston Ferrers, named Brixham Road, opened in 1861. But the proposal of the Dartmouth & Torbay Railway to terminate the line on the bank of the Dart at Greenway before spanning the estuary and proceeding along the west bank to Dartmouth was defeated in the House of Lords. It was 1864 before the last 6km (3¾ miles) to Kingswear, opposite Dartmouth and linked by a railway ferry across the river, was finally opened.

Built to broad gauge (2140mm/7ft 0¼in), the line was changed to standard gauge during an extraordinary weekend in May 1892, when 283km (177 miles) of line west of Exeter were converted. The

PAIGNTON & DARTMOUTH STEAM RAILWAY

Length of line: *11.2km (7 miles)*
Operating periods:
  Daily June–September; most of April and May;
  Tuesdays, Thursdays and Sundays in October.
Facilities: *Buffets, shops.*
Access for disabled: *Limited.*
Public transport: *Main line at Paignton.*
Nearby tourist attractions:
  Dartmouth Castle (EH),
  Bayard's Cove Fort (EH), Coleton Fishacre (NT).
Address:
  Queen's Park Station, Paignton,
  Devon TQ4 6AF.
Telephone (information): *01803 553760*
Telephone (timetable): *01803 555872*

line then settled into a familiar West Country pattern of heavy summer traffic and light carryings during the winter months. The growth of Torquay and Paignton as resorts ensured that the line was well-served by through trains or carriages from many parts of the country. The dining-car 'Torbay Express' was introduced in 1923, and in the summer of 1929 an all-Pullman train was introduced between London Paddington, Torquay and Paignton, taking 3 hours 40 minutes non-stop to Newton Abbot against the 3½ hours of the non-stop 'Torbay Limited'. The Pullman was not a success and ran for only two seasons.

The genesis of the Paignton & Dartmouth Steam Railway (PDSR) was the company that had saved what became the South Devon Railway between Buckfastleigh and Totnes (see page 79). In late 1972

➦GWR small-wheeled prairie tank No 4555 climbs away from the beach at Goodrington, providing passengers with panoramic views across Torbay.

◆The largest of several viaducts on the line is the 10-arch Greenway (or Maypool) Viaduct, which was built largely of hard limestone excavated from the adjacent tunnel.

it took over the section from Paignton to Kingswear, which British Rail (BR) intended to close. This is now the principal business of the Dart Valley Light Railway Plc.

A new station at Paignton was built, the track was modified, and some stock and locomotives were transferred from Buckfastleigh. Part of the rationale behind the PDSR was that, besides being a remarkably varied and attractive journey, the chronic traffic congestion of the area in summer makes the line a much more pleasant and quicker way of travelling between Torbay and Kingswear/Dartmouth. A connection with Railtrack at Paignton allows through excursions to operate.

Leaving the centrally sited station at Paignton, the train crosses Sands Road level-crossing and runs parallel with the Railtrack line to the carriage sidings at Goodrington. A crescendo of sound from the front end signifies the start of the 4-km (2½-mile) climb to Churston at gradients of 1 in 60–70. There are marvellous views over Torbay to the left, as well as various tourist attractions such as the water park and zoo. Two fine masonry viaducts follow, Broadsands and Hookhills, and the line turns inland to the former junction for the Brixham branch at Churston. On the approach, to the left, is a turntable and siding for maintenance wagons. The signal box and loop here are switched out except on the busiest weeks in July and August.

The character of the line changes dramatically as the train descends towards the 451m (495yd) long Greenway Tunnel. Steep hillsides carpeted with pasture or clothed in woodland enclose the line as the cutting sides steepen on the approach to the northern portal. Excavating the hard limestone of the tunnel was a difficult task, but it provided much of the stone for the gracefully curved 10-arched Greenway (or Maypool) Viaduct just beyond the southern portal, which marks another change in the landscape. The glorious spectacle of the Dart estuary opens up as the train descends at 1 in 60 towards the terminus, with views over the Britannia Royal Naval College and the picturesque town of Dartmouth on the opposite shore. Agatha Christie

lived at Greenway House from the 1930s until her death in 1976.

It was a peculiarity of the line that timetables always showed Dartmouth as the destination, and the GWR provided a station there. Its importance, despite the absence of a railway, was reflected in the higher grade of the stationmaster than his opposite number at Kingswear! In the days of steamships, Dartmouth was a rebunkering point, the coal being supplied by rail. When oil-firing took over, the movement was reversed – coal for Torquay gasworks and Newton Abbot power station was unloaded here and taken up the hill by rail.

Appropriately, the PDSR has five GWR steam locomotives: two 45XX 2-6-2 tanks, which were always associated with West Country branch lines, 4-6-0 No 7827 *Lydham Manor*, a powerful 2-8-0 tank, and a pannier tank. Most of the carriages are of early BR vintage but there is a Pullman observation coach that was used on the Southern Railway's short-lived 'Devon Belle' between London Waterloo and Ilfracombe.

➡Visible from Kingswear station is Dartmouth Castle, begun in the 14th century. It was one of the first castles to be designed with artillery in mind, and is opened to visitors by English Heritage.

Kingswear was the terminus of through expresses from London to Paddington. In September 1955, Castle class 4-6-0 No 5053 Earl Cairns leaves for London, with No 7029 Clun Castle in the foreground.

SEATON & DISTRICT ELECTRIC TRAMWAY

The scaled-down models of tramcars threading the Axe Valley in east Devon must be one of the most curious sights on a heritage railway, because almost all these lines have retained the gauge and broad appearance of operations before their closure by British Railways. This departure from normal practice is due to the passion of one man, Claude Lane, for tramcars.

In 1930 Lane founded a business in Barnet that made battery electric vehicles such as milk-floats and delivery vehicles. When demand fell after the Second World War, he diversified by opening passenger-carrying 375mm (15in) gauge lines operated by model tramcars at seaside resorts such as St Leonards and Rhyl. This was followed, most successfully, by a larger 610mm (2ft) gauge line at Eastbourne. In the mid-1960s, when road schemes in the Sussex resort threatened the tramway's tenure, Charles Lane began to look for a freehold site.

The railway closures of the Beeching era meant that there was no shortage of standard gauge railways for conversion into a narrow gauge tramcar route. Lane was impressed by the scenic attractions of the former Seaton to Seaton Junction line, and with support from Seaton council he won a public inquiry into the proposal to secure this former branch line of the London & South Western Railway (LSWR). Built by the briefly independent Seaton & Beer Railway and opened in 1868, the branch initially had a role in transporting locally extracted slate to the Home

↖*Seaton car No 7 is based on an open-topped design from the Llandudno & Colwyn Bay system, and like most of the tramcars was rebuilt in the Seaton workshops.*

Counties, but tourism soon became its mainstay. Through carriages to and from London Waterloo ran during the summer months, with up to 500 people arriving on Saturdays, prompting the Southern Railway (of which the LSWR became a part in 1922) to rebuild the station in 1937.

Construction of the line from the new depot at Seaton began as soon as all the equipment had been transferred from Eastbourne. The gauge was increased to 838mm (2ft 9in) and the first public train ran on 28 August 1970, using a trailer-mounted battery in the absence of an overhead wire. Tragically Claude Lane died the following year, but there were sufficient people to fulfil his vision, and the line has been gradually extended to its current length of 4.8km (3 miles) between the new elegant terminus in Seaton and Colyton. As well as the lovely scenery of the Axe Valley and the birdlife on the river, the tramway offers

SEATON & DISTRICT ELECTRIC TRAMWAY

Length of line: *4.8km (3 miles)*
Operating periods: *Daily April–November.*
Facilities: *Tea room, shops, children's playground.*
Access for disabled:
Special toilets at Seaton and Colyton; tramcar for 12 wheelchairs.
Public transport:
Bus from Axminster railway station.
Nearby tourist attractions:
East Devon Path crosses line, Pecorama, Shute Barton (NT).
Address:
Harbour Road, Seaton, Devon EX12 2NQ.
Website: *http://members.aol.com-seatrams*
E-mail address: *Seatrams@aol.com.*
Telephone (information): *01297 20375*

the opportunity to explore the historic villages of Colyford and Colyton. The latter has the country's last working tannery and the well-preserved church of St Andrew, with its extraordinary octagonal top storey on the crossing tower.

A large variety of tramcars operate the services, ranging from double-deck open-top and open-sided toast-rack vehicles in summer to fully enclosed cars for the cooler months. Many of the cars are literally cut-down full-size tramcars from which a section has been removed. All are based on prototypes drawn from all over Britain, recalling the all-too-brief era when all towns and cities had this pollution-free form of urban transport.

♦ Another open-top tramcar, No 2, was completed in 1964 and is based on an early 20th-century London Metropolitan design. Decoratively finished tram poles were once common.

♠ The attractive station at Ashburton would have been the terminus of the South Devon Railway had it not been for the A38 widening scheme. Here is GWR 0-4-2 tank No 1420 before hopes were dashed.

SOUTH DEVON RAILWAY

The three delightful Great Western Railway (GWR) branch lines that served small towns on the southern fringe of Dartmoor – Moreton-hampstead, Ashburton and Princetown – would all have made attractive preserved railways, but it was the shortest of the three that was chosen by a group of businessmen in 1962. The idea was to preserve the Totnes–Ashburton line in the style of a GWR branch, using employed staff supported by a volunteer association.

SOUTH DEVON RAILWAY

Length of line: *11.2km (7 miles)*
Operating periods:
  Almost daily April–September.
Facilities: *Buffet, shop, museum.*
Access for disabled: *Good.*
Public transport:
  Main line trains at Totnes; buses 188 from Newton Abbot to Buckfastleigh, X80 from Plymouth to Torquay, X38/9 from Exeter to Plymouth.
Nearby tourist attractions:
  Totnes Castle (EH), butterfly and otter centre at Buckfastleigh, Buckfast Abbey.
Address:
  Buckfastleigh Station, Buckfastleigh, Devon TQ11 0DZ.
Telephone (information): *01364 642338*

◄A characteristic Great Western branch line train was an 0-4-2 tank and an auto-coach or two, which enabled the locomotive to operate in either direction without running round its train.

The first section of the line, from Totnes to Buckfastleigh, was reopened in 1969 as the Dart Valley Railway (DVR). However, thanks to the short-sighted transport policies of the day, the line was severed north of Buckfastleigh in 1972 by the scar of the dual carriageway A38, and the Ministry of Transport refused to provide a bridge under the road to allow the line to continue to the Stannary town of Ashburton.

Curiously, Buckfastleigh was the intended terminus of the line's original promoters, because the prime objective of the broad gauge (2140mm/7ft 0¼in) Buckfastleigh, Totnes & South Devon Railway was the town's woollen mills rather than the diminishing tin traffic at Ashburton. However, before construction began it was agreed that the line would be extended to Ashburton, and the railway opened throughout in May 1872. Twenty years later it was converted to standard gauge (1435mm/4ft 8½in) during a weekend of Herculean effort when hundreds of miles of GWR broad gauge track were narrowed to conform to the rest of the country.

Goods traffic provided much greater revenue than the sparse passenger traffic, especially on fair days at Ashburton, where the modest capacity became so choked with cattle wagons that the shunting engine sometimes became boxed in. At Buckfastleigh the sidings and goods shed had to be expanded in 1906. Passenger traffic ceased in 1958 and goods services were withdrawn in 1962.

Although the DVR proved popular, revenue was insufficient to create a healthy balance sheet, given the reliance on paid staff. Accordingly the DVLR

concentrated its energies on the Paignton & Dartmouth Railway (see page 72) and the lease was handed over in 1991 to the South Devon Railway Trust, formed from one of the locomotive-owning companies with charitable status.

Before catching the train at Buckfastleigh, there is plenty to see. The railway museum in the former goods shed contains the only surviving broad gauge engine – vertical-boilered 0-4-0 No 151 *Tiny*, which was built for the South Devon Railway in 1868. It was withdrawn in 1883 and became a stationary boiler at Newton Abbot works until 1927, when it was placed on the station platform as an exhibit. It also includes

➨*On loan from Didcot Railway Centre, GWR 0-4-2 tank No 1466 at Staverton station, which has been used in the making of films and television programmes.*

what is thought to be the only surviving pigeon-carrying van, built to carry racing pigeons for release at a time when the railway ran whole trains of such vehicles for pigeon fanciers. The original signal box may be visited, and there are play areas and a maze near the picnic site on the banks of the River Dart, as well as a butterfly farm and otter sanctuary.

Leaping salmon may be seen in the Dart, the second river that the railway crosses after leaving the station, and swans and herons are often attracted to the river. River and railway are never far apart as the two share the valley down to Totnes. The cutting sides and river banks are ablaze with daffodils and primroses in spring. The river is to the right for most of the journey, so it is best to sit on that side. A sharp bend to the left brings the train past the stationmaster's house at Staverton and the loop that was put in soon after the line was reopened to allow a two-train service to operate.

Staverton station is so little changed that it has appeared frequently on film and television, notably and

A train on the South Devon Railway between Buckfastleigh and Staverton runs by the River Dart. The red and cream livery was an early British Railways colour scheme.

Before BR closed the Dart Valley line on 3 November 1958, GWR 0-4-2 tank No 1427 waits to leave Buckfastleigh with a train for Totnes. Most of the buildings were saved from demolition.

appropriately in the West Country tale, *The Hound of the Baskervilles*. Local cider was a principal traffic of the small goods shed beside the platform, and some local pubs still sell locally produced scrumpy. Staverton offers some good walks (a leaflet about them is available), and passengers can fortify themselves at the nearby inn dating from the 13th century, The Sea Trout.

A cutting soon after leaving Staverton once housed an air-raid shelter dug for King George VI when his train was stabled overnight during his wartime visits to the West Country. A glimpse may be had of Dartington Hall on the opposite bank. Two water pumping stations are passed before the train draws into the station at Totnes, where the station building came from Toller on the Bridport branch, the canopy from Axbridge in Somerset and the corrugated-iron stores hut from Bovey Tracey. For many years the station here was of little value as a means of public transport because there was no way of crossing the River Dart

The picturesque village of Corfe Castle was usually traffic clogged until the Swanage Railway and the park-and-ride at Norden helped to relieve pressure on the narrow streets.

SWANAGE RAILWAY

Length of line: *9.6km (6 miles)*
Operating periods: *Daily April–October.*
Facilities:
  Buffet, shop, exhibition and cinema coach (Norden).
Access for disabled:
  Access to shop and toilets; adapted coach
  on most trains.
Public transport:
  Buses from Bournemouth, Poole and Wareham
  to Swanage and Norden park-and-ride.
Nearby tourist attractions: *Corfe Castle (NT).*
Address:
  Station House, Swanage,
  Dorset BH19 1HB.
Telephone (information and timetable):
  01929 425800

to link the station with the town. Thanks to help from various councils, Dartmoor National Park and BR InterCity, sufficient funds were found to build the connection, and the footbridge opened in 1993.

The SDR has a fleet of former GWR locomotives ranging from the tiny branch line 0-4-2 tanks to a Hall class 4-6-0. Although most of the railway's carriages will be familiar to anyone who knew British Railways in the 1950s and 1960s, the SDR also has ten GWR coaches, notably the 1932 Ocean saloon *King George*, one of only eight luxurious vehicles built for the boat trains that operated between London and the docks of Plymouth.

SWANAGE RAILWAY

The Isle of Purbeck and the area around Poole Harbour were hardly affected by the early years of railway development and the broader commercial impetus it often engendered. As late as 1851 the population of Bournemouth was only 895, so it was hardly a prime target for railway promoters. It was not until May 1885 that the first public train left Swanage. The line had been built between Worgret Junction and Swanage by a local company that was soon taken over by the London & South Western Railway (LSWR), which operated the line from the outset.

Clay was a major traffic on the branch, and the industry's narrow gauge lines that threaded the Purbeck peninsula before the opening of the Swanage branch were quickly routed to exchange sidings with the standard gauge. But it was passenger traffic that flourished, augmented by heavy traffic connected with the annual summer army camps that were set up around Swanage to train volunteers. Five trains a day each way in 1885 grew to 19 up and 20 down trains a day by the 1950s, three of which had through coaches to London Waterloo. Military traffic during both world wars was heavy. In the Second World War, two 30.5cm (12in) rail-mounted howitzers were stationed on the branch, and the choice of Studland beach as a training ground for D-Day landings brought numerous troop trains, as well as special trains conveying King George VI, Winston Churchill, President Eisenhower and General Montgomery.

British Rail (BR) began moves to close the line to passengers in 1967, the last train running in January 1972. General freight had ceased in 1965, but the

opening of Wytch Farm oil terminal in 1978 meant that the section from Worgret Junction to Furzebrook would be kept open for oil and butane/propane trains, which are still operated by English Welsh & Scottish Railway. The Swanage Railway Society was formed in 1972 to reopen the line, despite the hasty lifting of the line by BR.

Few heritage railways have had their future determined by a referendum, but in 1975 one was held in Swanage to gauge the enthusiasm of the residents for the reopening of the line. The town

↑London & South Western Railway M7 0-4-4 tank No 30053 with a typical branch train is seen from the castle mound at Corfe with a train for Norden.

council owned the railway as far north as Northbrook bridge at the station throat and wanted to test opinion on whether it should allow the society to take over the station and railway. Eighty-three per cent voted in favour of reopening. Work began on restoring the various buildings at Swanage, and the first public train ran in 1979, albeit over a very short distance.

The real breakthrough came in 1986, when Dorset County Council voted unanimously to lease the trackbed between Swanage and Furzebrook to the Swanage Railway (SR). By summer 1995 trains were running over the 4.8km (3 miles) to Harman's Cross, and in August of that year trains were extended through Corfe Castle to the current terminus at Norden.

The SR has become an integral part of efforts by county and local councils to mitigate the effects of the appalling traffic congestion that afflicts the area on summer weekends. A park-and-ride has been set up at Norden to dissuade drivers from taking their cars into the immensely popular village of Corfe Castle, dominated by the Norman castle (NT). The scheme has been so successful that the car-park has had to be doubled in size. In due course the line will be rebuilt to link up with the surviving freight-only section of the branch at Furzebrook so that trains will run through to Wareham station to connect with main line services and encourage still more people to leave their cars at home.

The tiny building that forms the booking office at Norden station was once a crossing keeper's hut, from East Stoke on the Waterloo–Weymouth line. The lattice iron girder overbridge at the south end of the station once carried the clay-carrying Fayles Tramway over the line. The line descends through a cutting on to an embankment and stone viaduct, giving a fine view of Corfe Castle before arriving at the line's only original intermediate station.

A break of journey in one direction is almost mandatory: apart from the obvious attraction of the castle (discounted combined tickets are available on the railway), the village is one of the most pleasing in the county and has an exceptional hostelry in the 1549 Bankes Hotel. It is also worth visiting the station itself, which has been beautifully restored with a full-height booking hall and typical ladies' waiting-room. The goods shed has been converted into a museum, with a display of railway memorabilia and photographs of the line. The unusual signal box that once towered over the contiguous waiting shelter on the down

◀*Southern Railway unrebuilt Bulleid Pacific No 34072 257 Squadron leaves Corfe Castle with a train for Swanage. These locomotives were frequent visitors to the line with summer expresses.*

platform was closed in 1956 and replaced by a 12-lever frame in the porters' lobby on the up platform.

The line climbs steeply after leaving Corfe, summoning a sharper exhaust beat from the locomotive, and enters a stretch of rolling pastoral farmland fringed with bracken-covered hills. Harman's Cross has a passing loop controlled by a pretty LSWR-style signal box with stone base and wooden superstructure. Although the station was entirely built from scratch in the 1980s, it looks as though it is much older, helped by the Southern Railway concrete structures and fixtures made at its Exmouth Junction factory, which were such a feature of its modernized stations. It is also worth noting the superb quality of the masonry work on the line's many bridges, which were built for double track between Corfe Castle and Swanage.

The line drops down at 1 in 76 to the SR's first northern terminus and now a request stop at Herston, heralded by the Signal & Telegraph stores. Here you may have the first whiff of ozone from the sea as it wafts through open carriage windows – a smell that must have excited generations of holidaymakers as they neared their journey's end after a long train ride from distant parts of the country. The sight of locomotive parts denotes the large building on the Swanage Industrial Estate that the SR uses as its locomotive, carriage and wagon workshop. Playing fields on the left precede the small one-road engine shed and 15.24m (50ft) turntable rescued from Neasden in London, which are on the left. Just before the station buildings, on the right, is the goods shed that was almost doubled in length in 1937 when the station building itself was extended in matching stone.

For a line that will operate a service over almost 19.2km (12 miles) between Swanage and Wareham station, the SR has a relatively small fleet of

➤*Swanage station itself is little altered since this picture of the stock for a London Waterloo train with M7 0-4-4 tank No 30106 was taken in 1957, though the goods yard is now sadly a bus park.*

locomotives, with five that are well-suited to the task. Four are of classes that operated over the branch before the end of steam operation in 1967: LSWR M7 class 0-4-4 tank No 30053 of 1905, Southern Battle of Britain Pacific No 34072 *257 Squadron* and two BR 2-6-4 tanks. In addition there is a delightful Midland Railway half-cab 0-6-0 tank and a Great Western Railway 0-6-2 tank No 6695 that spent most of its life in the valleys of South Wales, a far cry from the rural delights of Purbeck.

WEST SOMERSET RAILWAY

Britain's longest preserved railway is the scenically delightful branch line that once linked the county town of Somerset with the resort and small fishing port of Minehead. Taunton is unfortunately not today's starting point for West Somerset Railway (WSR) trains, but a bus connects with most trains in both

▲ Double-headed Bulleid Pacifics were a rare sight, but one was re-created for a photographers' special in 1993 with No 34072 257 Squadron and No 34105 Swanage from the Mid-Hants.

directions at the southern terminus of Bishops Lydeard. Relying heavily on holiday traffic, the WSR has been one of the most innovative in finding ways of making it easy for visitors to do without their car. In this, it has been supported by local authorities and Exmoor National Park, both of which are anxious to reduce the impact of traffic congestion on the rural environment.

The first section of the line was built by the original West Somerset Railway and opened in 1862 as a broad gauge (2140mm/7ft 0¼in) railway between a junction with the West of England main line at Norton Fitzwarren, 3.2km (2 miles) west of Taunton, and Somerset's oldest commercial port at Watchet. It was a measure of the harbour's traffic

WEST SOMERSET RAILWAY

Length of line: *32km (20 miles)*

Operating periods: *Almost daily April–October.*

Facilities: *Buffets, shops, museums.*

Access for disabled:
Special toilet and level access at Minehead; special saloon coach takes 14 wheelchairs (advanced booking essential).

Public transport:
Southern National bus 28A links Taunton main line station with Bishops Lydeard, connecting with almost all WSR trains.

Nearby tourist attractions:
Bee World at Stogumber (combined tickets), Dunster Castle (NT), Cleeve Abbey (EH), start of South West Coast Path at Minehead.

Address:
The Railway Station, Minehead, Somerset TA24 5BG.

Telephone (information): *01643 704996*

Telephone (timetable): *01643 707650*

that it already had a railway: the standard gauge (1435mm/4ft 8½in) West Somerset Mineral Railway had opened in stages between 1857 and 1859 to bring iron ore from the Brendon Hills to the harbour for shipment to Ebbw Vale.

It was another 12 years before the section on to Minehead was opened by the independent Minehead Railway, although the entire line was worked by the Bristol & Exeter Railway, which became part of the Great Western Railway (GWR) in 1876. The line was converted from broad to standard gauge in 1882, but traffic remained light until after the First World War. Growing holiday traffic increased the number of trains in summer to the extent that the GWR doubled the track between Norton Fitzwarren and Bishops Lydeard and between Dunster and Minehead. It also added two passing loops, at Leigh Bridge near Stogumber and Kentsford near Watchet. The signal boxes were classified as 'Summer Posts' and switched

☛ *The Minehead branch was one of the last to be closed by British Rail in 1971. Hymek Bo-Bo No D7026 waits to leave Minehead with the 10.25 (Saturdays only) to London Paddington in 1970.*

out once the holiday excursion traffic subsided.

Although the opening of Butlins' holiday camp at Minehead in 1962 helped to increase traffic, the line was closed to passengers in 1971 (freight traffic had already ceased). The WSR was formed within a few months of closure to try to buy the line. In 1973 the county council had the foresight to buy the line, granting the WSR a 99-year lease of the line, which was reopened in stages from Minehead between 1976 and 1979. The question of access to Taunton has been

a perennial issue, thanks to the obduracy of British Rail (BR) when the signalling in the area was entirely replaced in the early 1980s. Instead of simply incorporating a relatively inexpensive point and utilizing the up relief line between Norton Fitzwarren and Taunton, BR ripped up this track and placed

➥*GWR 0-4-2 tank No 1450 threads the glorious countryside through which the West Somerset runs. More through trains from Railtrack will operate over the line in the 21st century.*

◆ A freight operated for the benefit of photographers passes through Bishops Lydeard station behind GWR small-wheeled prairie No 4561.

signalling equipment on the trackbed.

A basic connection does exist, but Railtrack limits through passenger running to just six trains a year. However, in 1997–8 the WSR benefited from the need to bring in 100,000 tonnes of armour stone to rebuild the sea defences at Minehead. To avoid tens of thousands of lorry movements, the decision was taken to bring it in by rail, so English Welsh & Scottish Railway operated the trains from Merehead quarries, with the WSR providing occasional steam assistance to the diesel on the steeper banks. This was the first time that a preserved railway had carried such a large volume of freight traffic.

The station at Bishops Lydeard has plenty to entertain waiting passengers before the start of their journey. The former goods shed is now a visitor centre with a working signal box and model railway, as well as space for displaying a locomotive or carriage. The line climbs for the next 6.4km (4 miles) up to the highest point on the line at Crowcombe Heathfield – the attractively restored station has featured in many television programmes and feature films. The small signal box was rebuilt with parts from boxes at Ebbw Vale and Frome.

From here the line descends to the sea, flanked by

➤ Skirting the sea near Doniford Beach Halt is one of West Somerset's most powerful locomotives, Somerset & Dorset Joint Railway 2-8-0 No 53808 (running as No 53807), built at Derby in 1925.

hills – the Quantocks to the right and the Brendon Hills to the left. The well-wooded station at Stogumber has become one of the busiest intermediate stations on the line, thanks to the recently established Bee World visitor centre and animal park. Combined tickets have encouraged so many holidaymakers to use the WSR to reach the centre that the two-coach platform is being extended to take six-coach trains. This has not been a simple operation: the lie of the land makes space here at such a premium that the GWR had to site the station building at a lower level than the platform, which is cut into a shelf on the hill.

The line crosses Woolston Moor and follows Doniford Brook down the valley to reach Williton, where operations are controlled from the last Bristol & Exeter Railway signal box in use, dating from the line's opening in 1862. This is also the depot for diesel locomotives based on the WSR. At the north end is an unusual barrel-roofed shed that was recovered from Swindon railway works. This early example of metal-framed pre-fabricated building is listed, and was re-erected thanks to the generosity of Tarmac Ltd. It is used for storage and as workshop space.

Turning sharply west and offering fine views over the sea, the train pauses at Doniford Beach Halt, a newly created stop for the nearby holiday complex. The concrete platform sections came from Monatcute

and the platform shelter was rescued from Cove on the Exe Valley line. The proximity of the railway to the sea allows passengers to appreciate the need for coastal defence work to prevent the cliffs being eroded.

A legacy of Watchet's 12 years as a terminus can be seen in the curious position of the station building, at right angles to the line. Conversations with sailors at the harbour are believed to have given Samuel Taylor Coleridge the inspiration for his famous poem *The Rime of the Ancient Mariner*. The trackbed of the West Somerset Mineral Railway offers a fascinating walk for anyone interested in industrial archaeology: the remains of the inclined plane and winding house can be seen, as well as the ruins of the mines and associated buildings. The station is sited in the town centre, which has many interesting historic buildings.

After extensive views over the Bristol Channel the line swings inland to Washford station, headquarters of the Somerset & Dorset Railway Trust, which has created in the station buildings a museum devoted to that popular cross-country railway. The yard is used by the Trust to restore and accommodate its rolling stock. It is only a 0.8-km (½-mile) walk from the station to the Cistercian abbey of Cleeve, which has remains from the 13th century, including some of the finest cloisters in England.

Returning to the coast down a 1 in 65 bank – the steepest on the line – the WSR reaches Blue Anchor station, where many passengers alight to enjoy the fine beaches nearby. The signal box has the last remaining level-crossing gate wheel in the West Country. A small museum of GWR artefacts may be visited in the station. Soon after leaving the station the castle of Dunster comes into view on the left, as well as more recent defensive works in the shape of Second World War pillboxes.

A long straight brings the railway to Dunster, where the listed station houses an Edmondson ticket press. This produces card tickets for other heritage railways as well as the WSR – a splendid example of an item of historical equipment finding a commercial use for the benefit of the railway. (Edmondson card tickets were the standard form of ticket between the 1840s and the 1980s, when they were superseded by

◀ A very popular place to visit from the WSR is the picturesque village of Dunster and its castle, the home of the Luttrell family for over 600 years and now owned by the National Trust.

▲ The picturesque setting of Crowcombe station is one of the most attractive on the line. GWR prairie No 4561 enters with a freight in 1994 before signalling of the station had been completed.

APTIS paper tickets.) The imposing castle that overlooks the village and its magnificent, medieval high street dates back to the 13th century, though it was extensively remodelled in 1868–72. For over 600 years the castle has been the home of the Luttrell family, who provided a large part of the capital to build the Minehead Railway – George Luttrell was the first chairman. A vintage bus linking the station and the castle runs on certain days.

Another long straight takes the line to Minehead across Dunster Marsh, passing on the right Butlin's Somerwest World Holiday Centre. The station is the headquarters of the railway, and the platform is the longest on a heritage railway, having been extended by the GWR between the world wars to accommodate 16-coach trains. The former goods shed has had to be pressed into service as the locomotive depot because the site of the original single-road shed and turntable to the south of the station building became a car-park.

The WSR has a representative collection of GWR locomotives, including no less than three Manor class 4-6-0s (built by BR in 1950), which are ideal engines for the line, and the Somerset & Dorset Trust saved one of the fine 2-8-0s built at Derby for the Bath–Bournemouth line. Two Southern Railway Pacifics, of Battle of Britain and West Country classes, will add the distinctive muffled exhaust of Bulleid's express engines to the sharper bark of Swindon's products.

CHAPTER 3
WALES

Wales is renowned for its narrow gauge railways.

The Ffestiniog Railway became a showcase for narrow gauge steam

locomotive developments, attracting emissaries of the Russian Tsar

as well as engineers fascinated by the technical progress made by this scenic

railway in the vastness of Snowdonia.

◆*Ffestiniog Railway Double Fairlie 0-4-4-0* **Merddin Emrys** *approaches Garnedd Tunnel. Built in 1879 at Boston Lodge, the engine is the oldest of the Double Fairlies.*

◆ *The Brecon Mountain Railway has provided one of the most splendid vehicles for people in wheelchairs – the caboose with birdcage window at the rear of this train.*

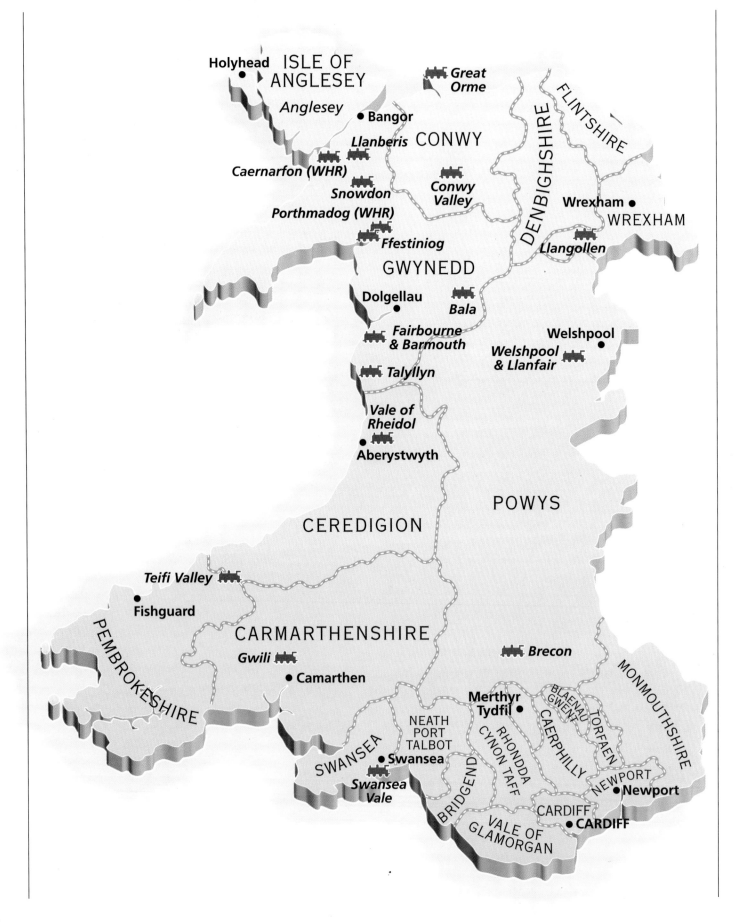

Holyhead ISLE OF ANGLESEY

Anglesey

Great Orme

• Bangor CONWY

Llanberis

FLINTSHIRE

Caernarfon (WHR)

Snowdon

DENBIGHSHIRE

Conwy Valley

Wrexham • WREXHAM

Porthmadog (WHR)

Ffestiniog

Llangollen

GWYNEDD

• Dolgellau

Bala

Fairbourne & Barmouth

Welshpool

Welshpool & Llanfair

Talyllyn

Vale of Rheidol

POWYS

• Aberystwyth

CEREDIGION

Teifi Valley

• Fishguard

PEMBROKESHIRE

CARMARTHENSHIRE

Gwili

• Camarthen

Brecon

MONMOUTHSHIRE

Merthyr Tydfil •

NEATH PORT TALBOT

BLAENAU GWENT

CAERPHILLY

TORFAEN

SWANSEA

• Swansea

Swansea Vale

BRIDGEND

RHONDDA CYNON TAFF

NEWPORT • Newport

CARDIFF • CARDIFF

VALE OF GLAMORGAN

BALA LAKE RAILWAY

Bala Lake, or Llyn Tegid, is Wales's largest natural lake, well known to fishermen as the only place where the gwyniad is found. This sparsely populated country may not have seemed promising territory for railway construction, but a delightful cross-country line between Ruabon and Barmouth Junction was opened in stages between 1861 and 1869. Built by independent companies, the line became part of the Great Western Railway (GWR) before the end of the 19th century. Although the line saw a healthy number of seasonal excursion trains, local traffic was light and most of the goods traffic was generated by Llangollen and Corwen. Passenger services were withdrawn in 1965 and the line between Llangollen and Barmouth closed completely.

The idea for the creation of a narrow gauge railway beside Bala Lake came from a local engineer, George Barnes. In 1971 he formed Rheilffordd Llyn Tegid Cyf (Bala Lake Railway Ltd [BLR]), which had the distinction of being the first company ever to be registered in the Welsh language. The proposal was supported by Merioneth County Council, which had the foresight to buy the entire trackbed. Equipment began arriving before the end of the year, and by Whit Monday 1972 the first section of the 600mm (1ft 11⅜in) BLR was opened to passengers. Gradual extensions brought the line to its present terminus at Penybont, 0.8km (½ mile) from the centre of Bala.

The principal station on the BLR and the location of the engine shed and workshops is Llanuwchllyn, which was a passing place before closure by British Railways. The station has been enlarged in a sympathetic manner by the BLR, including the addition of a second storey and a platform canopy that first sheltered passengers at Pwllheli before being moved to Aberdovey in 1909. The 1896 GWR signal box on the platform still controls points and signals – curiously, most are of Lancashire & Yorkshire Railway origin – and is often open to visitors.

The line hugs the lake shore for most of the journey, making the BLR one of the most scenic of Britain's tourist railways. Excessive flange wear is not one of the railway's problems, since the line is remarkably straight, with a dead-straight section of 2 km (1¼ miles) as it descends Ddolfawr bank at 1 in 70, eliciting a throaty beat from the tall-funnelled

◆ For a short distance from the terminus at Llanuwchllyn, the Bala Lake Railway runs through pastoral farmland with the Arenig Mountains in the distance to the north west.

BALA LAKE RAILWAY

Length of line: 7.2km (4½ miles)
Operating periods:
   Daily, early April–early October.
Facilities: Buffet, shop.
Access for disabled: Access to most trains.
Public transport:
   Gwynedd bus no 94 to Bala and Llanuwchllyn
   from Wrexham and Barmouth.
Nearby tourist attractions: Cyffdy Farm Park.
Address:
   Llanuwchllyn, Bala,
   Gwynedd LL23 7DD.
Telephone (information): 01678 540666

The Bala Lake's principal station, Llanuwchllyn, still has the original Great Western Railway station buildings and signal box. Hunslet 0-4-0ST Maid Marian *waits to leave for Bala.*

engines on the return. As the railway reaches the level of the foreshore, the imposing residence of Glanllyn Hall can be seen across the water. Now an outdoor activities centre, it was once the home of Sir Watkin Williams Wynne, who was a major shareholder in the railway and a director of the GWR. On his arrival by train at Glanllyn Halt, a flag was raised to summon a boat to carry him across the lake. This earned the Halt the nickname of Flag Station, the only GWR halt to be shown in the timetable by its nickname.

A series of halts that serve the many camping grounds along the lake punctuates the journey. One halt is at the passing loop at Llangower, from which there are some fine walks – short ambles to the pretty bay on the lake or longer hikes up the Glyn Valley. The

14th-century village church is passed on the right before the railway crosses the River Glyn by a twin-span bridge. The deepest cutting on the line takes the railway back to the lake, and after the halt at Bryn Hynod the line runs on a stone embankment right beside the water. Brightly coloured sails and canoes twist and turn across the lake with the Arenig Mountains as the spectacular backdrop.

A gentle curve to the right takes the railway under a road bridge to journey's end at Penybont, the site of the standard gauge Bala Lake Halt, which opened in 1934. A bay platform has been built to allow a mobile booking office and buffet to be stationed here on busy weekends and Bank Holidays.

Two of the BLR's steam locomotives come from the famous Dinorwic slate quarries at Llanberis. *Holy War* and *Maid Marian* were both built by Hunslet of Leeds, in 1902 and 1903 respectively, and the former was the last steam locomotive to work in a British slate quarry, her whistle falling silent in November 1967.

BRECON MOUNTAIN RAILWAY

Merthyr Tydfil is notable in railway history for being the place where an engine built by Richard Trevithick hauled the world's first steam train for a distance of 15km (9½ miles). It did this along the 1270mm (4ft 2in) tramway that linked Penydarren Ironworks with the Glamorganshire Canal at what became Abercynon. This portentous event reflected the industrial importance of South Wales, and it was not many decades later that the valleys of the area were laced with railways.

The section of the Brecon & Merthyr Tydfil Junction Railway between Brecon and Pant, to the north of Merthyr, was opened in 1863, but it was another five years before trains were running through to Newport. The northern part was an extraordinary railway with an 11.2-km (7-mile) bank at 1 in 38 up to the summit at the Beacon Tunnel, 609m (666yd) long and situated at 400m (1312ft) above sea level, making it the highest tunnel in the United Kingdom.

Hopefully the Brecon Mountain Railway (BMR) will one day run to a site near the northern portal of the tunnel. When the last goods train ran over the line in 1964, the track was lifted and the trackbed was overrun by sheep. However, the area's glorious, wild landscapes attracted Tony Hills, an engineer who was looking for a site for a narrow gauge railway. In 1976 planning permission was granted for a 610mm (2ft) gauge line over the 8.8km (5½ miles) north from Pant, past the site of the lonely station at Torpantau and through the tunnel. A proviso was that all journeys must start outside the Brecon Beacons National Park to reduce the number of cars in the park.

The line opened as far as the former junction at Pontsticill in 1980 and continued on to Dolygaer in 1995. Trains leave from the imposing three-storey station at Pant, close by an old railway tunnel

➤ *The superbly restored 0-6-2WT* **Graf Schwerin-Löwitz** *was built by Arn Jung in 1908 for the Mecklenburg–Pommersche Schmalspurbahn, north Germany.*

The Brecon & Merthyr line saw a large number of freight trains, many of them hauled by two pannier tanks. Nos 5793 and 4635 head a southbound freight through Pontsticill Junction in 1950.

ventilation shaft. The station incorporates the engine shed and workshops, which have a viewing area for visitors to watch restoration work on the impressive collection of engines from South Africa and east Germany as well as Britain.

The journey offers extensive views across the Taf Fechan Reservoir to the remains of quarries in the hills and mountains that are the constant backdrop to the west and north, the highest being Pen-y-Fan at 886m (2,847ft). On the outward journey the train passes through Pontsticill Junction, where the original signal box is now a holiday cottage. Passengers are not able to detrain at the temporary terminus at Dolygaer, but can break their journey on the way back at Pontsticill.

BRECON MOUNTAIN RAILWAY

Length of line: *5.6km (3½ miles)*
Operating periods:
  Daily mid-May–mid-September; Sundays late April–mid-May; Tuesday to Thursdays in October.
Facilities: *Buffet, shop.*
Access for disabled:
  Ramps, special toilets and carriage for wheelchairs.
Public transport:
  Merthyr railway station and bus to Pant Cemetery.
Nearby tourist attractions:
  Talybont reservoir.
Address:
  Pant Station, Dowlais,
  Merthyr Tydfil CF48 2UP.
Telephone (information): *01685 722988*

CONWY VALLEY RAILWAY MUSEUM

The picturesque Conwy Valley line between Llandudno Junction and the slate quarrying town of Blaenau Ffestiniog was one of the few branch lines in North Wales to survive the wholesale closures of the 1950s and 1960s. The philosopher Edmund Burke thought the valley 'the most charming spot in North Wales'. The section south of Llandudno to Llanwrst was opened to passengers in 1863 and continued on to Betws-y-coed in 1868. There, an imposing stone-built station was provided, and on former railway land opposite to it the Conwy Valley Railway Museum was set up.

The principal feature is the 184mm (7¼in) gauge railway, which weaves its way in and out of woodland to provide one of the longest runs on a railway of this gauge in Britain. It is operated by a variety of steam and petrol engines, ranging from a model of a late 19th-century Denver & Rio Grande wood-burning 2-8-0 to a Swiss 'Crocodile' electric. Alongside is an

◆Built by Milner Engineering in 1983, 184-mm (7¼-in) gauge Old Rube is based on one of the early 2-8-0s built for the mountain lines of the Denver & Rio Grande in Colorado.

CONWY VALLEY RAILWAY MUSEUM

Length of line: *2km (1¼ miles)*
Operating periods: *Daily Easter–end October.*
Facilities: *Buffet, shop, museum, model railway.*
Access for disabled: *Access to museum and toilets.*
Public transport: *Betws-y-coed station.*
Nearby tourist attractions:
   Penmachno Woollen Mill,
   Gwydyr Castle.
Address:
   The Old Goods Yard,
   Betws-y-coed, Gwynedd.
Telephone (information): *01690 710568*

◄ For a short period in the 1980s, before the Fairbourne was regauged, the 2-4-2 Siân ran in a rebuilt form as No 362 with an outline based on a Maine narrow gauge prototype.

electric 375mm (15in) gauge line operated by a replica of a tram car. At one point the two miniature gauges run alongside the standard gauge line.

Railway modellers will delight in the extensive railway based on continental practice and prototypes, as well as the dioramas re-creating scenes of the London & North Western Railway. A museum of railway memorabilia also includes an outstanding 375mm (15in) gauge model of a British Railways Britannia Pacific. A buffet coach that ran on the Southern Region still performs the same function,

standing alongside the oldest surviving Pullman vehicle in Britain.

FAIRBOURNE & BARMOUTH STEAM RAILWAY

The site of the Fairbourne & Barmouth Steam Railway (FBSR) is one of the most dramatic of any miniature railway. Built from a site close to Fairbourne station, it runs to the spit of sand opposite Barmouth, with magnificent views across the Mawddach Estuary and the wooden railway bridge to the summit of Cader Idris.

The Fairbourne Railway, as it was known until recently, has a long and fascinating history. Originally it was an industrial tramway built by Arthur

McDougall, of self-raising flour fame, to facilitate the construction of the resort of Fairbourne. When building work finished, it shuttled passengers to Penrhyn Point for the ferry to Barmouth.

In 1916 it was bought by the miniature railway company founded by W J Bassett-Lowke and converted to a 375mm (15in) gauge railway. Many engines came and went but the railway remained little changed in character until the mid-1980s, when it was regauged to 311mm (12¼in). Four half-sized models of 610mm (2ft) gauge prototypes operate the line, which has been extensively upgraded. The facilities have also been improved.

Ffestiniog Railway

The Ffestiniog Railway (FR) must be one of the best-known railways in the world. Millions of people have travelled on it in its preserved form, but even in its early years it was known by railway engineers across the world. Standing today on the platform at Porthmadog it is hard to imagine the scene

A mainstay of the Fairbourne Railway from the time of its construction by Bassett-Lowke in 1924 was the 4-4-2* Count Louis. *Today, the locomotive can be seen at Birmingham Railway Museum.

Fairbourne & Barmouth Steam Railway

Length of line: *4km (2½ miles)*
Operating periods: *Daily May–September.*
Facilities: *Buffet, shop.*
Access for disabled: *Limited.*
Public transport:
Fairbourne station (Gorsaf Newydd).
Nearby tourist attractions: *Castell-y-Bere.*
Address:
Beach Road, Fairbourne,
Gwynedd LL38 2PZ.
Telephone (information): *01341 250362*

that took place here in 1870, when emissaries of the Russian Tsar arrived to witness an important event in what was then still a remote corner of Wales (see below). Their presence reflected the pioneering features of the FR.

The railway indirectly owed its existence to an early job-creation scheme by a local landowner and the MP for Boston, William Madocks, to build the Cob across the Traeth Mawr estuary. This provided the means for the FR to cross the estuary to reach Blaenau Ffestiniog, and diverted the River Glaslyn, which scoured the estuary bed, to create a natural harbour (Port Madoc) that could be used by ships to collect the slate brought down from the mountains by the FR.

The appalling difficulty of transporting the slate extracted from the quarries around Blaenau encouraged the construction of the FR, which opened in 1836 using the gauge of 597mm (1ft 11½in) already adopted in the quarries. With a descending gradient of 1 in 80 from the quarries, the gauge was wide enough for horses to haul empty wagons up the hill, walking between the lines, and the gradient was steep enough for the wagons to descend by gravity with the horses riding in 'dandy' wagons.

The FR began to attract even wider attention when it commissioned four steam locomotives, the first for commercial use on such a small gauge. They arrived in 1863–4 in time to haul the first passenger trains over the line in 1865, the passengers being seated back-to-back along benches parallel with the rails to centralize the weight. But it was the next innovation that really grabbed the headlines. To haul heavier trains, the FR adopted a brilliant solution by the engineer Robert Fairlie. He produced a design for a double engine with boilers mounted back-to-back with central fireboxes, and each end of the locomotive was mounted on a pivoted powered bogie.

In 1870 trials of this revolutionary type of locomotive, which was given the name of its inventor, attracted many engineers, including the Imperial Russian Commission. It is hard to exaggerate the importance of this early foray into articulated locomotives, which led to colossal export orders for British industry over the next 80 years. The following

The 0-4-4-0T Earl of Merioneth was the first Fairlie to be built since 1911, being turned out of Boston Lodge works in 1979 with a boiler by Hunslet. It is seen here near Tanygrisiau.

*This 1956 picture of **Prince** was taken passing Boston Lodge. **Prince** was one of the first four engines and was built in 1863–4 by George England & Co at New Cross, London.*

FFESTINIOG RAILWAY

Length of line: *21.6km (13½ miles)*
Operating periods: *Daily March–November.*
Facilities: *Restaurant, shops, museum.*
Access for disabled:
Access to trains at Porthmadog and Blaenau Ffestiniog, by prior arrangement.
Public transport:
Minffordd and Blaenau Ffestiniog main line stations.
Nearby tourist attractions:
Llechwedd Slate Caverns, Gloddfa Ganol Slate Mine, Portmeirion.
Address:
Harbour Station, Porthmadog, Gwynedd LL49 9NF.
Internet address: *http://www.festrail.co.uk*
Telephone (information): *01766 512340*

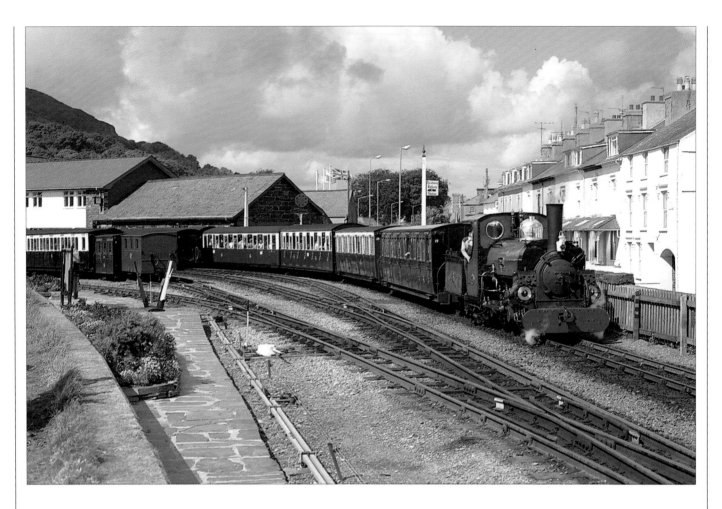

*The 2-4-0 saddle tank **Linda** began life as a 0-4-0ST, built by Hunslet in 1893 for the Penrhyn Quarry Railway. She was rebuilt as a 2-4-0ST in 1970 and is seen here leaving Porthmadog.*

year the FR produced another British 'first': bogie carriages, which employed an integral iron framing.

New roofing materials, and alternative means of taking the slates to their destinations without the need for double handling, combined to cause a gradual reduction in traffic and a correspondingly greater reliance on tourist traffic for the FR's lifeblood. But by the end of the Second World War, the track and rolling stock were in need of more money than the railway could find, and it closed abruptly in 1946.

The rescue of the derelict railway stemmed from a meeting in Bristol in 1951 and it is a story worthy of an entire book. The first public service ran in 1955 and the line has been gradually extended to a new station in Blaenau Ffestiniog alongside the terminus of the standard gauge line from Llandudno. To achieve this, an entirely new line, including a 262-m (287-yd) tunnel,

had to be built to circumvent the old formation, which had been flooded by an electricity pumped storage scheme. This attracted volunteers from all walks of life, some with scant interest in railways but fascinated by the challenge, which took 13 years from the cutting of the first sod in 1965. From Tanygrisiau, where the new line rejoined the old trackbed, the railway was pushed on to Blaenau Ffestiniog, services being restored in 1982, 31 years after that first meeting in Bristol.

With most of the railway situated in Snowdonia National Park, passengers enjoy one of the most scenically inspiring and varied rides of any heritage railway. The steadily rising gradient from sea level to 216m (710ft) means that locomotives have to work hard, a sound best appreciated from one of the open-sided carriages that are used in warm weather.

Trains leave from Harbour station in Porthmadog, which has changed remarkably little in its 160-plus years, curving right on to the long straight across Madocks' sea-fringed Cob. At the end, as the line turns sharply north and starts to climb, is Boston Lodge Works where all the locomotives and rolling stock are kept and maintained. It has even built new locomotives as well as carriages, so the construction dates of the FR's steam locomotives range from 1863 to 1992. Indeed, *Prince* has the distinction of being the oldest steam locomotive in the world still running on the line for which it was built.

As the train climbs to the first station at Minffordd, extensive views over Traeth Mawr (Great Sand) and Snowdonia open up to the left. Just before arrival at Minffordd, the standard gauge line from Shrewsbury to Pwllheli is crossed and the site of interchange sidings for slate traffic can be seen to the left. This is the closest station to the famous village of Portmeirion, created by the architect Sir Clough Williams-Ellis and setting for the cult 1960s television serial *The Prisoner*.

Climbing above the village of Penrhyn, where the FR has its volunteer hostel, the line enters more open country with good views over the valley of the River Dwyryd to the right. Past the crossing place at Rhiw Goch is the famous 19-m (62-ft) high stone embankment on which trains have been photographed since 1871, though it is now much more heavily wooded than 130 years ago.

The section before Tan-y-bwlch is exceptionally sinuous as the railway hugs the contours of the hills.

Down below beside the main road is the Oakley Arms Hotel, where the Russian delegation stayed in 1870, and the small lake known as Llyn Mawr, Mary's Lake. As the halfway point, the station at Tan-y-bwlch was laid out to allow trains of over 100 slate wagons to cross. It was here that Bessie Jones gained fame as the station mistress in the 1930s, dressed in Welsh costume and serving teas from the station house. As at most stations, there are plenty of good walks from the station, either through National Trust woodland or across moorland.

In the extensive views to the east of the Moelwyn Mountains, the bulk of the now defunct nuclear power station at Trawsfynydd can be seen. The attractive manor house below the line near Campbell's Platform was the home of Colonel Andrew Campbell, who helped to build the deviation beyond Ddaullt and had his own locomotive in a siding to pop down to Tan-y-bwlch (the road access is recent). The train describes a loop at Ddaullt, climbing to reach the new

➥*Taken in the early 1870s at Duffws, Blaenau Ffestiniog, this picture shows the early four-wheeled carriages.* **The Princess *was one of the first two locomotives to arrive on the FR, in 1863.***

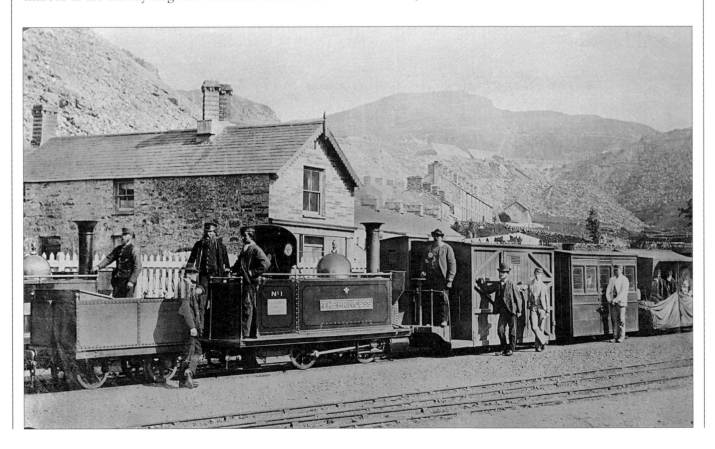

↞ *The village of Portmeirion is the unique creation of Clough Williams-Ellis, who from 1926 rescued threatened buildings and re-erected them in an enchanting coastal setting.*

Moelwyn Tunnel and, beyond, the Tanygrisiau Reservoir that flooded the old one.

Because of the deviation, there is a descent from Summit Cutting, opposite the lakeside Ffestiniog Power Station, down to the station at Tanygrisiau. As the train rounds the north-eastern end of the lake, with good views back over the lake, the line rejoins the old formation for the final section to Blaenau Ffestiniog. A visit to one or both of the slate mines should not be missed, for they place the FR in its context of a vibrant and fascinating industry and community.

GREAT ORME TRAMWAY

The Great Orme Tramway (GOT) is unique in Britain. It is the only street-running tramway operated by a cable running beneath paved sections of road and attached to cars by an endless rope that emerges through a central, slotted rail. The world's best-known system is probably that in San Francisco, and the only other example in Europe is in Lisbon.

The Great Orme is a vast headland of carboniferous limestone that rises to a height of 207m (679ft) above the town. Copper was once mined on its upper reaches, but it is better known for the curly horned wild goats, which are descended from a pair of the royal herd at Windsor that was released on the Orme in 1900. The GOT was built to allow the less energetic to reach the summit of

GREAT ORME TRAMWAY

Length of line: *1.6km (1 mile)*
Operating periods: *Daily Easter–October.*
Facilities: *Shop.*
Access for disabled: *Limited.*
Public transport: *Llandudno main line station.*
Nearby tourist attractions:
   Great Orme Mine, Bronze Age Heritage Centre.
Address:
   Victoria Station, Church Walks,
   Llandudno.
Telephone (information): *01492 574229*

the Great Orme and enjoy its rich flora and birdlife, as well as the views. The tramway opened in 1902–3.

The two-section tramway did not have an easy start: corner-cutting and parsimony during its construction made operations unreliable, and the Motherwell-built cars were left in the open for lack of covered accommodation, those on the upper section sometimes blowing over in fierce winds when standing empty. In 1932 a fatal accident prompted a major overhaul of the tramway. Now owned by Conwy County Borough Council, the GOT has recently benefited from further investment.

☛ *The first street-running section of the Great Orme Tramway is unique to Britain, its haulage cables running under the track like similar systems in San Francisco and Lisbon.*

On loan from the Severn Valley Railway, GWR small-wheeled prairie No 4566 passes the level crossing and signal box at Bronwydd Arms station on the Gwili Railway.

The tramway begins at Victoria station, a delightful period structure of 1904 named after a hotel that once stood on the site. Trams rise through the terraced streets that formed the old village of Llandudno before it became a fashionable resort during the mid-Victorian years. At Black Gate the GOT reaches a dedicated route beside the road, and views along the coast soon open up as the tramcar passes its descending counterpart. At the halfway winding house (both were converted from steam to electricity in 1957–8), passengers disembark and walk along the platform to a car on the upper section, on which there are again two tramcars. However, they are hauled by exposed cables guided by pulleys, similar to the numerous funicular systems of Switzerland.

Entering an area designated a country park in 1980, the line crosses the road leading to the 12th-century St Tudno's church. At the summit are shops and a café, and a visitor centre for the country park.

GWILI RAILWAY

The Gwili Railway (GR) has been rebuilt along the trackbed of one of the Great Western Railway's (GWR) most attractive cross-country routes, linking the towns of Carmarthen and Aberystwyth. It took three hours to cover the 90km (56 miles), trains calling at most of the 21 intermediate stations or halts. The central section used the valley of the Teifi, but the 13.2-km (8¼-mile) section being rebuilt by the GR crosses the River Gwili no less than eight times.

The original broad gauge (2140mm/7ft 0¼in) line was built by two railway companies – the Carmarthen & Cardigan and the Manchester & Milford. The first never reached Cardigan and the second linked neither of the towns in its title. The line opened in stages between 1860 and 1867, though it was 1906 before through trains between Aberystwyth and Carmarthen ran, with the acquisition of both companies by the GWR.

Passenger traffic from such a sparsely populated region was never heavy, despite through holiday excursions and the opening of tourist stops such as Caradog Falls Halt. Withdrawal of passenger services was planned for February 1965, but was hastened by a flood in 1964, which severed the line at Llanilar. Creameries kept the southern part of the line open for freight until 1973, when the last milk tanks headed south.

The GR was formed in 1975, but managed to secure only 0.8km (1 mile) of track north from Bronwydd Arms station before British Rail (BR) insisted on removing the rest. However, they obtained freehold of the trackbed over the 13.2km (8¼ miles) between Abergwili Junction outside Carmarthen and Llanpumpsaint. The first trains ran in 1978 and the limit of operations has been gradually extended to give longer rides.

All journeys start at Bronwydd Arms, where all the buildings have had to be re-erected by the GR. The superbly built signal box came from Llandybie on the Central Wales line and the station building was made up from parts of Llandovery North signal box and Ammanford Town station. Refreshments are provided by an experimental 1960s BR conversion, intended as a pattern for future catering vehicles, which was used predominantly on the Cambridge Buffet Express.

Leaving the station, the engine has to tackle a 1 in 60 gradient that eases to almost level as passengers are offered their first view of the river on the right. The train passes through a landscape of rolling hills generously covered in trees and woods, finally entering a sharp left-hand curve to reach Llwyfan Cerrig station. This was the site of a quarry that loaded stone at a siding and also provided the material to build today's platform, on which the station building of 1911 from Felin Fach on the Aberaeron branch has been re-erected and faithfully restored to evoke memories of bygone railway travel. A miniature

GWILI RAILWAY

Length of line: *2.4km (1 1/2 miles)*
Operating periods:
*Sundays in May; Wednesdays and Sundays
in June; Wednesdays, Saturdays and Sundays in July;
daily in August; Sundays in September.*
Facilities: *Buffet, shop.*
Access for disabled: *Limited.*
Nearby tourist attractions:
*Carmarthenshire Museum (Abergwili),
Gwili Pottery.*
Public transport:
*Carmarthen main line station and then buses
460, 461 and 462.*
Address:
*Bronwydd Arms Station, Bronwydd Arms,
Carmarthenshire SA33 6HT.*
Telephone (information): *01267 230666*

◀*Built by Hunslet in 1889 and bought by the Bala Lake in
1969, 0-4-0 saddle tank* **Elidir** *was delivered to Dinorwic
Quarry as* **Enid,** *after the highest gallery in the quarry.*

railway operates here on some days, and there is a walk
through the trees that now mask the old quarry. The
line is being gradually extended north, though there
will be no access to trains from any temporary
platforms, and south to reach a new terminus beside
the Carmarthen bypass.

The GR has a wide variety of industrial
locomotives and it loans main line locomotives from
other heritage railways and museums. Its most
distinguished item of rolling stock is the Taff Vale
Railway third-class brake of 1891, the body of which
was found in a field in Herefordshire and restored by
pupils of a Bridgend school. It has even appeared on
television in *Blue Peter*.

LLANBERIS LAKE RAILWAY

Beside the southern terminus of the Llanberis Lake
Railway (LLR) at Gilfach Ddu is the Welsh Slate
Museum. An hour or two at the museum followed by a
walk along the woodland and quarry trails, taking in a
restored cable incline and a ride on the LLR, provide

an excellent introduction to the economic and social
impact of the slate industry on this magnificent area of
North Wales. Its importance is indicated by the number
of men who worked at the Dinorwic Quarries alone –
over 3,000 at the peak of its prosperity.

The LLR uses the trackbed of the Padarn Railway,
which was built to take slate from the Dinorwic
Quarries to waiting ships at Port Dinorwic on the
Menai Strait. First opened in 1824 as a horse-drawn
610mm (2ft) tramway, it was converted to 1220mm
(4ft) gauge by 1843, with steam operation beginning
six years later. The lines in the galleries of the quarry
remained at the smaller gauge, so the 1220mm (4ft)
gauge carried the small wagons of slates piggyback
fashion to avoid the need for transhipment.

The LLR is laid to a gauge of 600mm (1ft 11⅝)
and was opened to passengers in 1971, with an

▶*The BLR runs along the lake shore for most of its length.
Besides salmon and coarse fish, the lake contains a rare char
named the Tor Goch. Gulls, swans, ducks and heron can also
be seen.*

⬥*Visitors to the Welsh Slate Museum at Llanberis can see demonstrations of old machinery, forges, a foundry, saw mill and water wheel as well as explanatory films.*

LLANBERIS LAKE RAILWAY

Length of line: *3.2km (2 miles)*
Operating periods:
  Mondays to Thursdays in March and October;
  Mondays to Fridays in April; Sundays to Fridays
  from May to September.
Facilities: *Buffet, shop.*
Access for disabled:
  Level approaches to shop, café and train; special
  toilets; carriage for wheelchairs.
Nearby tourist attractions:
  Welsh Slate Museum, Padarn Country Park,
  Dolbadarn Castle, Snowdon Mountain Railway.
Address:
  Gilfach Ddu, Llanberis,
  Gwynedd LL55 4TY.
Telephone (information): *01286 870549*

extension to the present terminus at Penllyn the following year. Trains are worked by three slightly regauged Hunslet tank engines that worked in Dinorwic Quarries and date from 1889 to 1922.

Leaving Gilfach Ddu, the train passes through an arch dating from 1900 over which waste was taken from the Vivian Quarry for tipping at the lake shore, which the railway parallels throughout its length. With glorious views across the lake to Snowdon and the surrounding peaks on the left, and glimpses of slate workings amid the woods on the right, it is a delightful journey. The return journey may be broken at the halfway station of Cei Llydan, where Cwm Derwen Woodland Centre has an audio-visual display and an adventure playground as well as woodland walks.

LLANGOLLEN RAILWAY

The Llangollen Railway (LR) is based on the same cross-country route as the Bala Lake Railway (see page 99) – the wonderfully scenic line that linked Ruabon and Barmouth. Built by four separate companies, all but the Dolgelley to Barmouth section became part of the Great Western Railway (GWR) before the end of the 19th century. At 87.2km (54½ miles), it was one of the longest such lines, calling for the use of tender locomotives rather than tank engines on most trains. Most of the stations served villages that can seldom have provided more than half a dozen passengers for each train, if that, but the towns of Llangollen, Corwen and Dolgellau generated substantial passenger and goods traffic.

The railway from Ruabon to Llangollen was opened in 1862 and reached Corwen, the target of the LR, three years later. Queen Victoria arrived at the station for a visit to the area in 1889, and the line hit the headlines in 1945 when the Llangollen Canal burst its banks and swept the railway embankment away, but neither the signal nor telegraph wires were cut. A mail train fell into the breach and caught fire.

Goods traffic west of Llangollen was re-routed in 1964 and all passenger services were withdrawn the following year, goods traffic between Ruabon and Llangollen lingering until 1968.

It is hard to believe that there was not a foot of track on the entire line when the LR Society was able to take over Llangollen station in 1975 thanks to the foresight of Merioneth County Council in buying the line on closure. Fund-raising for track was slow until a generous gift of surplus track from a Shell refinery enabled significant progress to be made. The first section reopened in 1981, and Carrog, the current western terminus, was reached in 1996.

➣Taken in 1964 before the Ruabon–Barmouth line closed to passengers, this picture from the footplate of No 7827 **Lydham Manor** *shows the three-span bridge over the Dee at Pentrefelin.*

◀BR-built 4-6-0 No 7822 **Foxcote Manor** *leaves Berwyn for Carrog, with the suspension bridge on the left. No 7822 worked over the line while based at Chester shed during the 1950s.*

Few railway stations in a town the size of Llangollen can match its picturesque setting, right on the bank of the River Dee and overlooked by well-wooded hills and the ruins of Castell Dinas Bran. It is indicative of the scenic delights to come. The platforms are much longer than required by local traffic, having been extended to cope with visitors. The footbridge has a most unusual arrangement in that it is extended through the upper level of the station building to reach the pavement of Abbey Road behind the station, which is at a higher level than the platforms.

Leaving Llangollen the line enters a deep cutting until the River Dee comes into view on the left. Sidings on the right lead to the higher level goods yard that now acts as the railway's engine shed and workshop area. On

➦A special train from Butlins' holiday camp near Pwllheli passes through Llangollen behind pannier tank No 9669 and an unidentified Manor class 4-6-0 in September 1954.

LLANGOLLEN RAILWAY

Length of line: *12km (7½ miles)*
Operating periods:
  Most weekends throughout the year; daily May–October.
Facilities: *Buffet, shop.*
Access for disabled:
  Access to shop and toilets at Llangollen; to toilets at Glyndyfrdwy and Carrog; special coach to wheelchairs.
Public transport:
  Ruabon station, then hourly Bryn Melyn bus.
Nearby tourist attractions:
  Pontcysyllte Aqueduct, Valle Crucis Abbey, Llangollen Canal Horse Drawn Boat Centre, Plas Newydd.
Address:
  The Station, Abbey Road, Llangollen, Denbighshire LL20 8SN.
Telephone (information): *01978 860979*
Telephone (timetable): *01978 860951*

the left-hand side is Llangollen Goods Junction signal box, newly built on the site of the original using a lever frame from Ruabon. The line between Ruabon and Llangollen Goods Junction was doubled in about 1900, reflecting the importance of the town's traffic. Above the line on the right is the Llangollen Canal, a feeder of the Shropshire Union Canal.

The sidings at Pentrefelin were put in both for the exchange of slates between canal and railway and for the many rakes of carriages that would have to be stored during the Eisteddfod, in readiness for the returning crowds. This useful area of land was relaid in 1981 for storage and is the site of the LR's new carriage shed; its nucleus is being formed by the remains of No 9 shop from Swindon railway works. The railway curves to the left to cross the Dee by a

A demonstration freight train for photographers is captured near Glyndyfrdwy behind BR 2-6-0 No 76079, built at Horwich in 1957 and based for most of its life at Sutton Oak.

three-span bridge. The grade steepens to 1 in 80, requiring hard work from the engine. Hillsides and trees close in on the railway as it approaches the first station at Berwyn, overlooking the river and the famous chain bridge. The building is in mock Tudor style and compares favourably with the ugly hotel on the opposite bank. A 10-minute walk from the station brings you to Telford's artificial Horseshoe Falls of 1800, designed to act as a feeder for the canal.

The line crosses a road and stream by a six-arch stone bridge and enters a cutting. To the right the falls can be glimpsed as the line runs along the contour of the hillside, with fine views to the right, and the stone-built Llantysilio Hall and mountains behind. This house was once home to the Beyer family, renowned throughout the world for the Manchester-built locomotives under the name Beyer Peacock. With a whistle the train plunges into Berwyn Tunnel, 630m (689 yards) long, emerging to more spectacular views before the request stop and passing loop at

Deeside Halt, from where footpaths lead down through meadows to the river.

The valley broadens before the next station at Glyndyfrdwy, heralded by much whistling for the level-crossing gates. Because the station is a private house, the wooden booking-on office from Northwich engine shed was transplanted to serve as the booking office and waiting room. The footbridge came from Welshpool. Behind the children's playground on the left can be seen the remains of the inclined plane that brought slate down for transhipment until closure of the quarry in 1960. The GWR signal box beside the crossing came from Leaton on the Chester–Shrewsbury line, and there is a café on the eastbound platform.

Just when you think the scenery can't get any better, it does, with delightful views over the moors, river and mountains beyond. Fly fishermen in waders and wildfowl populate the river. After cantering along one of the few straight sections on the LR, the train reaches the current terminus at Carrog, situated in tranquil and much more open countryside. The station was reopened by the Duke of Westminster in 1996 and has a waiting room open to the rafters with an attractive fireplace, and a café. The attention to detail in re-creating the station has even extended to part of the cattle dock. A leaflet of suggested walks is available.

▲ Snowdon Mountain Railway No 3 **Yr Wyddfa** *pauses at Clogwyn before the final section of the climb to the summit. No 3 was built in Winterthur, Switzerland in 1895.*

The LR's objective is to reach Corwen and provide a second passenger base to compare with Llangollen, though the money required means that it is likely to be a few years into the new millennium before the people of Corwen hear a steam whistle again.

The LR has a good selection of GWR locomotives, though many are still at various stages of restoration after their sojourn in the sea air of Barry scrapyard in South Wales. Already serviceable are Manor class 4-6-0 No 7822 *Foxcote Manor*, a pannier and a prairie tank.

SNOWDON MOUNTAIN RAILWAY

The Snowdon Mountain Railway (SMR), constructed in the 1890s, has enabled millions to enjoy the breathtaking – often literally in high wind – views from the summit. The idea for a railway up Snowdon appears to have come from an almost off-the-cuff remark by that most fearsome of Victorian railway chairman, Sir Richard Moon. When his London & North Western Railway opened the branch from Caernarfon to Llanberis in 1869 he said, 'The

◀ The only structures of any size on the SMR are the Lower Viaduct of 14 arches, part of which is seen here, and the four arches of the Upper Viaduct.

next extension must be to the top of Snowdon.'

The rack technology to scale mountains was largely developed by the Swiss, with a little inspiration from the United States. Of the four rack systems named after their inventors – Abt, Riggenbach, Strub and Locher – the Snowdon Mountain Tramroad and Hotels Co Ltd chose the first. Roman Abt's system has two, or even three, parallel toothed plates with staggered teeth and gaps so that a pinion on the locomotive is always engaged in a gap in the rack rails mounted centrally between the two running rails. This naturally made it much safer than a single rack rail. However, it was not to save the SMR from a catastrophe.

Construction began in 1894 to a gauge of 800mm (2ft 7½in), the 7.5-km (4½-mile) single-track route being split into four sections by three passing loops. Five 0-4-2 tank locomotives were ordered from the Swiss Locomotive and Machine Works in Wintherthur, which is still building rack steam locomotives, and the opening day was set for Easter Monday, 6 April 1896.

On the first downhill run, near Clogwyn, the pinions on locomotive No 1 *LADAS* (based on the initials of the landowner's wife) became disengaged from the rack, left the rails and plunged down the mountainside, ending up as an irreparable wreck. On seeing the crew jump to safety, two passengers followed suit and one died of his injuries.

The railway closed while an investigation was carried out. It was decided that the tragedy was caused by slight subsidence due to ice melting under the newly laid and packed track, rather than any fault of the rack system. None the less, gripper-girders were attached to each side of the rack bars and these were engaged by angled grippers fitted to the locomotives and carriages. The SMR has operated safely ever since, helped by its elaborate braking systems and the usual mountain railway practice of locomotives propelling rather than pulling coaches.

The station building at Llanberis is the original, and the track is the only level section on the entire line. Thereafter the line climbs at an average gradient of 1 in 7.8, with the steepest part at 1 in 5.5. Two viaducts, of 14 and 4 arches, are crossed soon after leaving the station, and a waterfall crashing into the River Hwch can be seen to the left.

The railway enters open moorland after Waterfall station, the abandoned farm buildings being houses

➤ Little has changed in the appearance of steam-hauled trains on the Snowdon Mountain Railway, although new rolling stock has been built. This shot was taken in 1954.

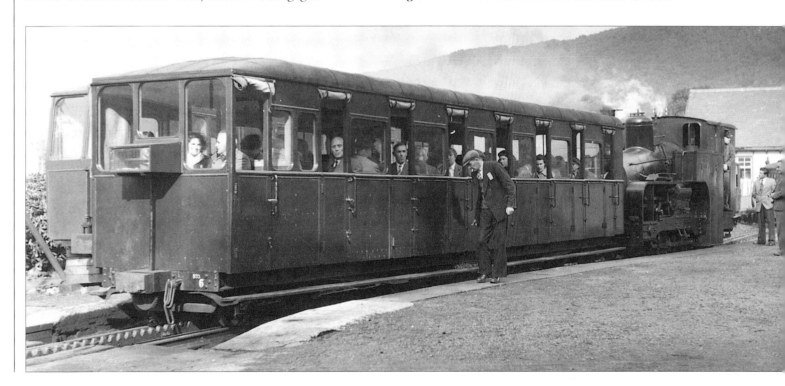

SNOWDON MOUNTAIN RAILWAY

Length of line: *7.6km (4⅝ miles)*
Operating periods: *Daily mid-March–October.*
Facilities: *Buffet, shops.*
Access for disabled: *Limited.*
Public transport:
Bangor station bus to Caernarfon and local bus to Llanberis; Snowdon Sherpa services from Betws-y-coed.
Nearby tourist attractions:
Welsh Slate Museum, Padarn Country Park, Dolbadarn Castle, Llanberis Lake Railway.
Address:
Llanberis,
Gwynedd LL55 4TY.
Telephone (information): *01286 870223*

once used during summer grazing. To the left is the ruin of Dolbadarn Castle, thought to have been erected by Llywelyn the Great in the 13th century. Snowdon is first glimpsed on the long straight approach to Hebron station, named after a disused chapel nearby. The walkers' path runs alongside the railway as far as the prosaically named station at Halfway, where the steam engines take water.

After Rocky Valley, the trains negotiate the spine of a ridge that gives stupendous views down both sides of the mountain. In the days of obligatory headgear, so many hats were made airborne at this point that it was known by locals as the 'valley of hats'. The station at Clogwyn, or even Rocky Valley, may have to be journey's end when wind speeds make it unwise to

The two tanks built for the Talyllyn Railway by Fletcher Jennings at Whitehaven in 1865–6 were of different design. Though built as a 0-4-0, No 1 Talyllyn was rebuilt as an 0-4-2 saddle tank, seen here at Wharf in 1959.

proceed higher. As the train makes an assault on the steepest part of the climb, passengers can see as far as the Isle of Man and even the Furness peninsula on a clear day.

Yet the summit of Snowdon itself remains hidden until a brow is reached and it comes suddenly into view. The final approach to Britain's highest station at 1065m (3494ft) is along a rocky edge. It is only a few minutes' walk to the summit at 1085m (3560ft), which is just as well as the demand for seats on the SMR is such that passengers are guaranteed a seat only on the train by which they ascended: it waits at the summit for 30 minutes before returning. Out of the peak season, however, there should be little difficulty in spending longer at the peak and taking refreshment at the summit building. The first structure was built in 1895 and replaced in 1936 by a building designed by Clough Williams-Ellis, which itself had to be extensively rebuilt in 1984–6.

Of the SMR's fleet of seven steam locomotives (three more were built in 1922–3), five are serviceable. They are supplemented by four Hunslet diesel locomotives and three diesel-electric railcars built in Tredegar.

TALYLLYN RAILWAY

The Talyllyn Railway (TR) will always have a special place in the pantheon of heritage railways because it was the first in the world to be rescued by volunteers, and showed that it was possible for a group of like-minded enthusiasts to make a commercial success of railway preservation, thanks, of course, to untold hours of unpaid labour.

It all began in October 1950 with a meeting at the Imperial Hotel in Birmingham, to which anyone who was known to have any interest in the TR was invited. The meeting was prompted by the death of the railway's owner, Sir Henry Hadyn Jones. He had also owned the Bryn Eglwys Quarry, which the TR was built to serve, but the decline of the slate trade forced their closure in 1946. Sir Henry, by then over 80, promised to keep the railway open during his lifetime and ran a service on three days a week during the summer months.

▶ 0-4-0 well tank No 2 Dolgoch is caught near Nant Gwernol in woods typical of the Afon Fathew valley. The TR is operated by six steam locomotives, the youngest built in 1949.

At the Birmingham meeting the room was full and the outcome was the formation of the Talyllyn Railway Preservation Society (TRPS). Doubtless out of a sense of loyalty to her husband's love of the railway rather than any conviction that the rescue attempt would be successful, Lady Haydn Jones handed the line over to the TRPS. Although much of the railway was in a parlous state, trains were run as far as Rhydyronen in 1951. There is no better record of the struggle to preserve any railway than L T C Rolt's

TALYLLYN RAILWAY

Length of line: *11.6km (7¼ miles)*
Operating periods: *Daily April–October.*
Facilities: *Buffet, shops, museum.*
Access for disabled:
 Special toilets and access to shop and café at both Tywyn and Abergynolwyn; new carriage for wheelchairs.
Public transport: *Tywyn station.*
Nearby tourist attractions:
 Castell y Bere, Dolgoch Falls.
Address:
 Wharf Station, Tywyn,
 Gwynedd LL36 9EY.
Telephone (information): *01654 710472*

▶*0-4-2 saddle tank No 1* **Talyllyn** *among the daffodils at Rhydyronen. The engine has been returned to its early lettering and appearance for the benefit of photographers.*

book about the TR, *Railway Adventure*, written with his customary feeling for industrial history. Had the TRPS failed in its objectives, it is unlikely that many of the railways in this book would have been saved, for it was the example of the TR that inspired others to follow in its footsteps.

The original TR opened in 1866 to bring slate down from Bryn Eglwys Quarry, at the end of an inclined plane from the railway's eastern terminus at Nant Gwernol, to the standard gauge at Towyn (now Tywyn). Built to a gauge of 686mm (2ft 3in), the TR was operated by two dissimilar tank engines built by Fletcher Jennings of Whitehaven, *Talyllyn* and *Dolgoch*. Both were built as 0-4-0 saddle tanks, but *Talyllyn* was soon rebuilt as an 0-4-2 to improve its rough ride. Traffic reflected the Festiniog Railway's experience: as slate traffic gradually declined, passenger numbers through tourism grew.

The name of the TR's station in Tywyn, Wharf, commemorates the interchange sidings between the two gauges. The station building was once the goods office, and the nearby Narrow Gauge Railway Museum provides a good introduction to a type of railway that has exercised a particular fascination for generations of railway enthusiasts.

The lower falls at Dolgoch are close to the station, but a couple of hours or more should be allowed to reach the top of the gorge. A leaflet describing the walk is available.

Passengers quickly notice that TR carriages have doors on one side only, a precaution advised by the 1866 Board of Trade inspector who was concerned at the risk from the limited clearances on the line. Leaving Wharf station, the train – always powered by steam because the TR eschews diesels for public trains – heads through a flower-filled cutting to reach the first station at Pendre, closer to the town centre than Wharf. Pendre has always been the locomotive and engineering base of the railway, and there is also a large carriage shed.

A succession of hills lie ahead as the line enters open country along the shoulder of the hillside on the southern flank of the Afon Fathew valley, which the railway climbs all the way. Slate or stone fences and hedges flank the railway to keep out the sheep, but in spring lambing time the train occasionally has to stop for the driver and fireman to catch and reunite an errant lamb with its mother.

Past the ash-sheltered station at Rhydyronen with its slate shelter, the hills begin to close in and more trees screen the line, though there are still wonderful views of Cader Idris ahead. In high summer, trains sometimes cross at the loop provided at Brynglas station, near which there used to be a fulling mill. A deep cutting after the station was afflicted by poor drainage and was given the name Tadpole Cutting because it was so often full of frogspawn in the spring.

An attractive wood heralds the principal engineering work on the line, the three-arched bridge that spans Dolgoch stream, and this is followed by the station, where many passengers break the journey to visit the nearby falls. Water tanks allow the engines to replenish their supplies – immortalized by Terence Cuneo's painting of the station when the rhododendrons are in flower. There is no loop at this station but trains can cross shortly after Dolgoch, at Quarry Siding, which supplied ballast for the TR.

Abergynolwyn was the destination of all passenger trains of the pre-preservation TR and for many years the terminus of the rebuilt TR, but in 1976 working was extended to Nant Gwernol, where wagons used to be taken up to the quarries by the Alltwyllt inclined plane. Horses were always used to move wagons around in the quarry. This last section passes through beautiful, dense woodland bisected by paths and forestry tracks, once the site of the TR's first engine shed. There was also an incline down which supplies to the village of Abergynolwyn were lowered, having been transhipped at Towyn. There are footpaths through the woods from Nant Gwernol, as well as a path up to Bryn Eglwys Quarry.

The success of the TR meant that more engines were soon needed to operate sufficient trains to cope with demand. Fortunately, two Corris Railway locomotives were stored at Machynlleth, and the TR was able to buy them from British Railways for £25 each. They were named *Sir Haydn* and *Edward Thomas*. In 1953 the TR was given an Andrew Barclay 0-4-0

tank named *Douglas* after its donor, Douglas Abelson. Then in 1991 another Barclay tank, a former 900mm (3ft) gauge engine built for the Irish Turf Board, entered service as *Tom Rolt*.

A delightful picture of the Talyllyn in the 1920s with No 2 Dolgoch at Dolgoch station with the attractive water tower on the left, which has been restored to its original appearance.

TEIFI VALLEY RAILWAY

The Teifi Valley Railway (TVR) starts from the site of Henllan station on the Pencader–Newcastle Emlyn branch of the Great Western Railway (GWR), which opened throughout as late as 1895. Serving sparsely populated countryside, it is little wonder that passenger services were withdrawn in 1952, long before the Beeching era. Freight, however, lingered until 1973, thanks to milk traffic.

There was nothing left at Henllan but two platforms and a hut when the TVR took over the site in 1981. Since then the trackbed has been cleared of vegetation, drainage reinstated, bridges refurbished and track laid to a gauge of 610mm (2ft) to reach the terminus at Llandyfriog. The TVR opened its doors in

TEIFI VALLEY RAILWAY

Length of line: *2.8km (1¾ miles)*
Operating periods: *Good Friday–October.*
Facilities: *Buffet, shop, play areas, miniature railway.*
Access for disabled: *Special coach, ramps and toilets.*
Public transport:
    Carmarthen station and bus 461 to Henllan.
Nearby tourist attractions:
    Cilgerran Castle (NT).
Address:
    Henllan Station, Llandysul,
    Pembrokeshire SA44 5TD.
Telephone (information): *01559 371077*

1986. Paths have been created to take passengers to scenic places on the river and a nature trail has been opened at Henllan.

The line follows the river valley through heavily wooded countryside and negotiates the gorge through which the Afon Cynllo flows on its way to join the Teifi. A panoramic view of the valley opens up to the south before journey's end.

Steam trains are hauled by a Hunslet 0-4-0 saddle tank of 1894 from Penrhyn slate quarry and the attractive 0-6-2 tank built by Kerr Stuart in 1918.

◆*Built by Hunslet in 1894, 0-4-0 saddle tank* **Alan George** *was used at Penrhyn quarries. The open cab must have been unpleasant when working in torrential rain.*

◆ *Cilgerran Castle stands on the west bank of the River Teifi. The ruinous 13th-century castle inspired Turner, Richard Wilson and Pieter de Wint, and is cared for by the National Trust.*

VALE OF RHEIDOL RAILWAY

Opened in 1902, the 597mm (1ft 11½in) gauge Vale of Rheidol Railway (VRR) had the distinction of being the last part of British Rail (BR) to be operated by steam. BR inherited the VRR when the railways were nationalized, and the success of the railway meant that any moves by BR to rid itself of this anomalous undertaking were scotched by widespread opposition. Consequently the VRR survived long after the end of BR steam operations in

VALE OF RHEIDOL RAILWAY

Length of line: *18.8km (11¼ miles)*
Operating periods: *Easter, May–October.*
Facilities: *Buffet, shop.*
Access for disabled: *Limited.*
Public transport: *Aberystwyth station.*
Nearby tourist attractions:
Llywernog Silver Lead Mine, Aberystwyth Castle.
Address:
The Locomotive Shed, Park Avenue, Aberystwyth, Cardiganshire SY23 1PG.
Telephone (information): *01970 625819*

1968, in fact until the decision to sell it in 1988.

The line's history goes back to 1897, when the independent Vale of Rheidol Light Railway was authorized to build an 18.8-km (11¾-mile) line between Aberystwyth and Devil's Bridge. Interestingly, in the light of the growing popularity of the Welsh slate railways at this time, the VRR was built as much with tourists in mind as the lead ore deposits at Devil's Bridge. These generated only 20 tonnes of ore a day and closed altogether during the 1920s, whereas over 1000 passengers a day used the line during the Easter

➥ *The three 2–6–2 tanks of the Vale of Rheidol Railway were the last steam locomotives to be operated by British Rail. No 9* **Prince of Wales** *dates from 1902, but was rebuilt in 1924.*

The last rays of sun illuminate the station at Devil's Bridge as one of the Davies & Metcalfe 2-6-2 tanks runs round its train in the 1950s.

holiday in 1903. It is therefore no wonder that the VRR was the first narrow gauge railway to concentrate on tourist traffic, closing during the winter months from 1931.

The GWR invested in the line, closing the first, isolated station in Aberystwyth and re-routing the line to terminate alongside the standard gauge station, while most of the rolling stock was replaced shortly before the Second World War. Closure of the line down to Carmarthen allowed narrow gauge tracks to be laid into the platform at Aberystwyth used by that service, making the connection between gauges even easier.

The purchaser in 1989 was Tony Hills of the Brecon Mountain Railway (see page 101). Now under different ownership, a passing loop has been installed and the arrears of maintenance made good.

Leaving Aberystwyth the train passes on the left the VRR locomotive shed, which is the former standard gauge depot, built in 1938 and closed in 1965. This is large enough to accommodate much of the VRR's

☛2-6-2 tank No 9 **Prince of Wales** *rounds a curve on the approach to Devil's Bridge. The wooded nature of the scenic part of the line allows for few open photographic positions.*

rolling stock during the winter months. Keeping company for a mile or so with the standard gauge line to Machynlleth and Shrewsbury, the VRR sets out across the flood plain of the River Rheidol. Crossing the river, the line heads for the southern flank of the valley, which it climbs on gradients as steep as 1 in 40 through the woods, raising echoes from the locomotive's sharp exhaust beat.

The drop to the valley floor below becomes progressively more impressive, squealing flanges testifying to the short radius of the curves that open up new views with each twist and turn. The seven intermediate stations and halts were relegated in status during BR days, but Nantyronen has remained a stop for water. Beyond Aberffrwd the drops become

precipitate and the views even more spectacular, especially in spring and autumn when the leaf cover is not too dense.

The line enters more open terrain with steep-sided cuttings and passes through a nature reserve before arriving at Devil's Bridge. Three bridges, dating from the 11th century, 1708 and 1901, cross the River Mynach one above the other. Beneath them is the Devil's Punchbowl, fashioned by the pounding water over the millennia. Opposite the entrance to the Punchbowl is the path to the Mynach Falls, which cascade through a wooded gorge. A circular walk can be made, returning to the road via the Robbers' Cave.

Trains are operated by the three 2-6-2 tanks built by the GWR for the line in 1923–4 to replace the locomotives it inherited from the previous owner. They were converted to oil-firing following the drought of 1976, to minimize the risk of fire in the woods.

WELSH HIGHLAND RAILWAY (CAERNARFON)

The reconstruction of this remarkable 40-km (25-mile) narrow gauge railway is one of the most exciting tourism projects in Britain. At the time of writing, the verdict of a public enquiry is awaited – the outcome will determine whether or not Rheilffordd Eryi/The Welsh Highland Railway, Caernarfon (WHR) will be allowed to extend beyond Dinas along the old trackbed into Snowdonia National Park to reach Porthmadog. For the sake of sustainable tourism and ridding the national park of at least some of its excessive motor traffic, it is hoped that the WHR will be given the go ahead.

The first section of the Welsh Highland Railway to be reopened starts from a station at Caernarfon close to the immense fortress built by Edward I overlooking the estuary.

The railway through the Aberglaslyn Pass was one of the most spectacular sections of narrow gauge railway in Britain. In time, trains will run through it again.

The original WHR was an extraordinary line. It opened as late as 1922, a time when slate traffic was already declining and competition from road traffic was eroding rail revenues. Incorporating and extending two separate, impecunious 597mm (1ft 11½in) gauge railways, the WHR completed the route between Dinas Junction, where it connected with the London & North Western Railway (LNWR) branch from Caernarfon to Afon Wen, and Porthmadog to connect with the Festiniog Railway. The WHR struggled from the start, and in 1927 the receivers had to be called in. There was not enough money to bring the locomotives up to a reliable standard, and high fares deterred passengers. The last passenger train ran in 1936, and goods traffic ended the following year.

The first part of the new WHR opened in late 1997, utilizing the trackbed of the LNWR between Caernarfon and Dinas. The initiative is being driven forward by a separate organization under the wing of the Ffestiniog Railway. It is operated by Beyer Garratt locomotives built in Manchester and repatriated from South Africa.

WELSH HIGHLAND RAILWAY (CAERNARFON)

Length of line: *4.8km (3 miles)*
Operating periods:
Daily, early April –early November.
Facilities: *Small shop.*
Access for disabled:
Ramp for disabled to gain access to train.
Public transport:
Regular bus service from Bangor station.
Nearby tourist attractions:
Caernarfon Castle (Cadw).
Address:
Harbour Station, Porthmadog,
Gwynedd LL49 9NF.
Telephone (information): *01766 512340*

The line begins within an arrow shot of Caernarfon Castle. Beside the new terminus is the former Union Works of de Winton, which until 1902 produced distinctive locomotives with vertical boilers and two vertical cylinders alongside. They were designed for narrow gauge quarry lines, and one example survives in use on the Leighton Buzzard Railway (see page 34). The line runs through pleasant pastoral landscapes with enticing views of the distant mountains, into which the railway will, hopefully, one day take both visitors and local passengers.

The WHR already has a new Pullman car named *Bodysgallen* after the hotel owned by the carriage's sponsor Historic Hotels Ltd. The vehicle was built by Winson Engineering and entered service in September 1998.

WELSH HIGHLAND RAILWAY (PORTHMADOG)

The short section of the old Welsh Highland Railway (WHR) reopened from the south-western end of the original railway, adjacent to the main line station in Porthmadog, has been the work of

◀ *The power of the former South African Beyer Garratt 2-6-2+2-6-2s, which have been rebuilt for the Welsh Highland Railway, will be useful on the steep sections in Snowdonia.*

WELSH HIGHLAND RAILWAY (PORTHMADOG)

Length of line: *1.2km (¾ mile)*
Operating periods: *Easter; May–October.*
Facilities: *Buffet, shop, shed tours.*
Access for disabled: *Special toilets, access to trains.*
Public transport: *Porthmadog station.*
Nearby tourist attractions:
   Llechwedd Slate Caverns,
   Gloddfa Ganol Slate Mine, Portmeirion.
Address:
   Gelert's Farm Works, Madoc Street West,
   Porthmadog LL49 9DY.
Telephone (information): *01766 513402*

a separate organization from the WHR, Caernarfon, but they are now working together towards the common objective of rebuilding the railway.

The trains run from Porthmadog to Pen-y-Mount and a journey can include tours of Gelert's Farm Works, which provide a good introduction to both the WHR and the challenges and trials of restoring steam locomotives.

The most historic engine in the collection of five steam locomotives based here is the 2-6-2 tank *Russell*, which was built by Hunslet of Leeds in 1906 for what became the southern constituent of the WHR, the

☛*Thankfully, the restoration of the 1906-built 2-6-2 tank* **Russell** *has entailed restoring its attractive original appearance. It was mutilated to work on the FR, but was still too big for the Moelwyn Tunnel.*

Portmadoc, Beddgelert & South Snowdon Railway. However, she was delivered to Dinas and operated on the northern portion of the future WHR, the North Wales Narrow Gauge Railway. *Russell*'s attractive profile was ruined at Boston Lodge works so that she could work over the Festiniog Railway (FR); someone's calculations were wrong, and she stuck in Moelwyn Tunnel. Although no further attempt was made to work *Russell* over the FR, the engine retained the cut-down chimney, dome and cab until rebuilt by the WHR.

WELSHPOOL & LLANFAIR LIGHT RAILWAY

The Welshpool & Llanfair Light Railway (WLLR) was a very unusual type of railway in Britain, a narrow gauge railway built for general traffic – the overwhelming majority of narrow gauge railways in Britain were associated with the extraction of a specific mineral.

*▲ The Welshpool & Llanfair was operated by two Beyer Peacock-built 0-6-0 tanks. No 823 **Countess** is captured amid the lovely mid-Wales scenery with a special mixed goods train.*

In common with a number of standard gauge as well as narrow gauge lines, the impetus for its construction was the Light Railways Act of 1896. This was intended to make railways cheaper to build by reducing certain obligations in exchange for speed and weight restrictions.

Opened in 1903, the WLLR was operated by the Cambrian Railways, which owned the main line through Welshpool until 1923 when the Great Western Railway (GWR) took over. Unsurprisingly passenger services were withdrawn in 1931, but carriage of the staple goods traffic – building materials, coal, agricultural supplies, sheep and cattle, continued until 1956.

The line became the first to be taken over from British Railways, enabling the inaugural public passenger train to run in 1963. Problems over redevelopment and road crossings regrettably made it impossible to retain the section through the streets and backs of Welshpool, so the other terminus at Llanfair Caereinion became the base from which the WLLR has been gradually reopened. The last section from Sylfaen to Welshpool Raven Square carried its first fare-paying passengers in 1981.

The character of the Banwy valley through which the railway runs seems to have remained remarkably unspoilt by the 20th century, apart from the traffic on the parallel A458, thankfully out of sight for most of the journey. Great care has been taken to preserve the light railway character of the line, and the original

➥ In 1953 traffic in Welshpool is interrupted by 0-6-0 tank No 822 as it threads through the streets. Common on the Continent, such tolerance of street railways was rare in Britain.

buildings at Llanfair have been sensitively restored or incorporated into extensions to improve the amenities.

The views from the carriage windows offer a series of constantly changing panoramas of delightful hilly farmland backed by deciduous woods on the upper contours, as the line turns this way and that to avoid having to cross the river. Sometimes this was unavoidable, and the river crossing a mile or so out of Llanfair nearly spelt disaster in 1964, when floods severely damaged the three-span bridge. As on many heritage railways since, a branch of the armed services came to the rescue and undertook its repair as a training exercise.

The intermediate stations are little more than short platforms and a hut, though a signal box was put up at Castle Caereinion in 1907 with the intention of crossing passenger trains here, though the necessary signals were never installed. The steep contours are

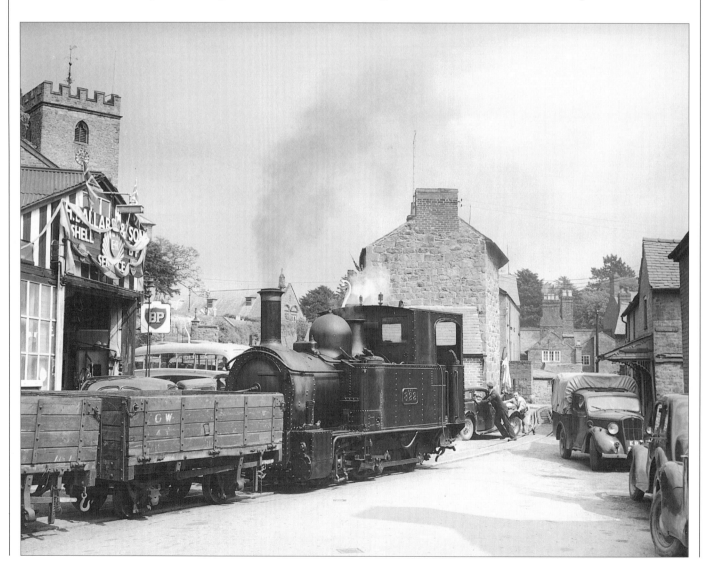

reflected in the railway's gradients, which are as steep as 1 in 24 and include a mile at 1 in 29 as the line drops down to Welshpool from the line's summit near Sylfaen. The station building at Welshpool was rescued from Eardisley on the Midland Railway and is much more in keeping with the railway's atmosphere than the rather raw red-brick signal box.

Trains are operated by a cosmopolitan selection of locomotives, drawn from Antigua, Austria, Finland, Scotland and Sierra Leone as well as the two pretty engines built for the opening of the line by Beyer Peacock. They were named *The Earl* and *The Countess* after the Earl and Countess of Powis, who provided much of the land on which the WLLR was built.

☛*One of the WLLR imports is a German Military Field Railway 0-8-0 built by Franco-Belge at Raismes in France and later used on the Styrian Local Government Railways in Austria.*

WELSHPOOL & LLANFAIR LIGHT RAILWAY

Length of line: *12.8km (8 miles)*
Operating periods:
  Daily mid-July–early September; weekends and Bank Holidays early April–September.
Facilities: *Buffet, shop.*
Access for disabled:
  Easy access to shop; coach for wheelchairs; special toilet at Welshpool.
Public transport: *Welshpool station.*
Nearby tourist attractions: *Powys Castle (NT).*
Address:
  The Station, Llanfair Caereinion SY21 0SF.
Telephone (information): *01938 810441*

CHAPTER 4
THE MIDLANDS & EAST ANGLIA

The region has the only heritage railway in Britain that sets out to convey the atmosphere of the main line steam railway, with double track, goods loops and industrial sidings.

◄*Midland Railway Trust Class 8F 48151 passes a fine MR signal as it departs from Butterley Station. Butterley itself is famous for its ironworks.*

◄*Trains that pass at speed or overtake a goods train in a loop are unique to the Great Central Railway. LMS 0-6-0 No 4422 (alias No 44598) is seen passing Swithland signal box.*

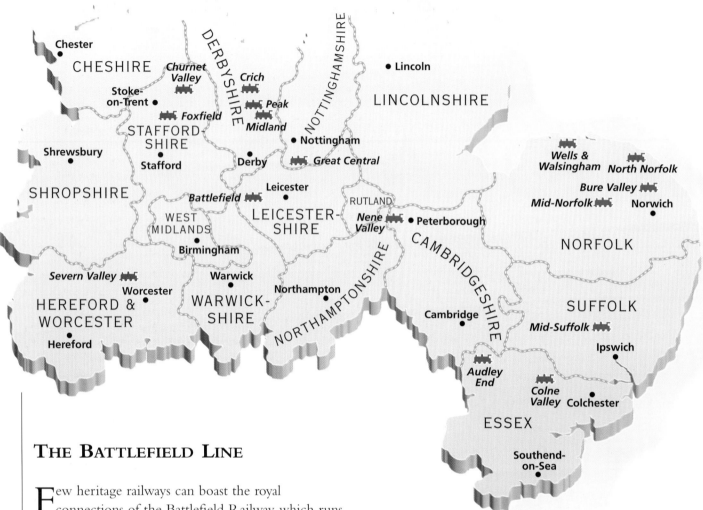

THE BATTLEFIELD LINE

Few heritage railways can boast the royal connections of the Battlefield Railway, which runs through pleasant Leicestershire farmland between Shackerstone (Junction) and Shenton. The royal associations are separated by 400 years. Over an area to the east of the railway at Shenton, now divided into several fields and fringed by woodland, the concluding battle of the Wars of the Roses was fought out in 1485, when Richard III became the last king of England to be killed in battle, at Bosworth Field.

During the first decade of the 20th century, Shackerstone Junction was the destination of the royal train bringing Edward VII to visit Lord and Lady Howe at nearby Gopsall Hall, to which there was a carriage drive from the station. The house itself was built in the 1750s for Charles Jennens, who selected the words from the Bible for Handel's *Messiah*. Handel himself was a frequent guest and composed music here, such as the hymn tune 'Gopsall'. The house was torn down in 1951.

The railway that brought the king to Gopsall was opened in 1873 and was known as the Ashby &

Nuneaton Joint Railway, reflecting its joint ownership by the London & North Western and Midland railways. It was a Y-shaped route, with Moira and Coalville (near Ashby-de-la-Zouch) as the two northern points, Nuneaton at the south and Shackerstone Junction at the fork of the lines. Freight, particularly coal, was always more important than passenger traffic, which came to an end as early as 1931, though excursions continued to use the line until the 1960s. The Coalville branch shut in 1964 and the Moira–Nuneaton line closed with the last freight train in 1970.

The Shackerstone Railway Society (SRS) was formed in 1969 and has gradually restored the line south, reopening to Market Bosworth in 1978 and to Shenton in 1992. Despite the interval of 47 years between closure to passengers and reopening, the SRS was fortunate that the station building at Shackerstone was still intact.

The headquarters of the railway is at the tranquil village of Shackerstone, where the goods yard has become the locomotive and carriage workshop and depot. The attractive station building with pronounced eaves houses a traditional booking office (which still has its blackout material from the Second World War), café and museum, which is stuffed with railway memorabilia, much of it associated with lines in the East Midlands. Doubtless as a result of its early closure, Shackerstone station never had mains water and electricity until the SRS took over. Unusually the footbridge was built to perpetuate an existing right of way across the line, and is a solid brick and girder structure that continues on the east side to join a footpath across the fields.

Leaving Shackerstone along a formation built for double track, trains pass a newly built signal box (the original by the junction had been demolished before

☛ The special atmosphere of the steam railway at night has encouraged many railways to set up photography sessions. On loan from Birmingham Railway Museum, 0-6-0PT No 7752 stands at Shackerstone.

the SRS took over) using a Midland upper section on an inauthentic brick base. The frame is of North Staffordshire Railway origin, from Uttoxeter. The

THE BATTLEFIELD LINE

Length of line: *8km (4½ miles)*
Operating periods:
  Weekends and Bank Holidays mid-March–October; midweek railcar Wednesdays in June, July and August.
Facilities: *Buffet, shop, museum.*
Access for disabled: *Limited.*
Public transport: *None.*
Nearby tourist attractions:
  Bosworth Battlefield, Twycross Zoo.
Address:
  Shackerstone Station, Shackerstone, Nuneaton CV13 6NW.
Telephone (information): *0116 291 7460*
Telephone (timetable): *01827 880754*

Some railways, like the Battlefield Steam Railway, rely largely on locomotives that worked for industrial companies rather than on former main line engines, like this example at Market Bosworth.

railway's engine depot is passed on the right as the railway enters well-wooded country with beautifully kept hedgerows through which trees have been allowed to grow. Pheasants are a common sight.

Keeping company with the railway throughout the journey is the Ashby Canal, which can be seen on a parallel course to the right. Although the railway destroyed much of the canal's traffic, it is still used by pleasure craft and there is a delightful walk known as the Ashby Canal Trail. Before long the railway emerges on an embankment and for much of the way to Shenton the train offers elevated views over attractive, gently rolling countryside peppered with distant spires and clusters of farm buildings.

A massive timber yard on the right heralds the approach to Market Bosworth station, which is situated to the west of the architecturally fascinating town that gave its name to the battle. Although the train stops here, the occupation of the principal building by a garage has prevented the SRS from restoring the station as it would wish. At the south-west corner of the platforms is an attractive London & North Western signal box that controlled the station and goods yard, now full of rolling stock awaiting restoration.

More extensive panoramas to east and west enable passengers to see the countryside across which the Plantagenet and Tudor armies marched to confront each other around Ambion Hill. This is the hill to the east of the southern terminus at Shenton station, where the attractive building on the eastern platform was recovered from Leicester Humberstone Road.

From the platform there is a pleasant, waymarked walk over the battlefield with periodic information boards describing the various stages of the battle and relating it to the scene before you. For a fuller account of this crucial battle that changed the tide of English history, the Battlefield Visitor Centre on the course of the walk gives a deeper insight into the event and its context. It also has a shop and tea room.

The Battlefield Railway's fleet of steam locomotives is made up entirely of industrials, most of which are not really up to providing passenger services over a line of this length. Consequently the railway often hires engines from other heritage railways. It also has a few main line diesel locomotives that operate some services.

BURE VALLEY RAILWAY

One of the longest miniature railways in the country, built to a gauge of 375mm (15in), links the capital of the Norfolk Broads at Wroxham with the market town of Aylsham, a distance of 14.4km (9 miles). Opened in 1990, the Bure Valley Railway (BVR) is the most ambitious new miniature railway to have been built in Britain since the Second World War.

The railway is built on the trackbed of the former East Norfolk Railway, from a junction with the Norwich–Cromer line at Wroxham to Aylsham. It was opened in 1879–80, and two years later the East Norfolk was taken over by the Great Eastern Railway (GER), which extended the line on to a junction with the Dereham–Wells line at County School (see page 160). It was never a busy line, and the last passenger trains ran in 1952 to the accompaniment of Chopin's Funeral March at Aylsham station, which was wreathed in black crêpe paper. Goods traffic kept the line open until 1982, and two years later the track was lifted.

That might have been the end of the railway, with the trackbed gradually being built over or returned to fields in the usual way, and thus precluding any possibility of reopening. Thankfully wiser councils prevailed, quite literally. Reflecting the enterprising vision with which a good number of East Anglian district and county councils are blessed, the idea of using the trackbed between Wroxham and Aylsham for a miniature railway developed into a joint venture between Broadland District Council and the BVR. In 1989 the Council bought the trackbed and split it into two longitudinally, leasing one half to the BVR for 125 years and creating a footpath known as the Bure Valley Way, parallel to the proposed railway on the other half.

Not since the construction of the Romney, Hythe & Dymchurch Railway had a miniature railway been built on this scale. Contributions to the £2.5 million project were made by the English Tourist Board and the Department of the Environment, enabling the railway to be built and opened to the public only a year after work began.

Although miniature in gauge, there is nothing Lilliputian about the capabilities of this railway: its trains can carry up to 250 people, and its carriages even have electric heating as well as lighting, for which Santa Special passengers are very grateful. It is operated mostly by steam locomotives ranging from a 2-6-4 tank engine named *Wroxham Broad*, appropriately finished in the glorious garter blue of the GER, to a pair of 2-6-2s based on the ZB design of narrow gauge locomotive on Indian Railways, about 100 of which were built for export by British locomotive builders.

It is only a short walk from the Railtrack station at Wroxham to the BVR station, where a turntable is provided. There is quite a climb out of the station as the train turns west away from the Cromer line on the right, producing a staccato bark from the locomotive that is echoed off the sides of the first cutting. Fields of sugar beet, which once provided some of the old railway freight traffic, flank the line, and the thatched

A bus service links the Bure Valley station at Aylsham with nearby Blickling Hall (NT), the early 17th-century mansion of the Hobarts and putative birthplace of Anne Boleyn.

▲ Bure Valley No 4 (formerly Siân) has left the railway since this picture was taken, showing the engine after its American outline was removed on leaving the Fairbourne (see page 104).

barn of Grange Farm can be seen on the left.

A brick bridge spans the line on the approach to the station at Coltishall, a village made famous by the airfield built in 1940 that was home to Squadron Leader Douglas Bader's 242 Squadron and now the base for three RAF Jaguar squadrons. Intermediate stations are request stops, so the driver needs to be warned if you want to break the journey. After about 2km (1¼ miles) the lovely Elizabethan Little Hautbois Hall stands beside the line, on the south side, though its blocked-up windows are regrettable reminders of the infamous window tax.

A stretch beside the River Bure may produce the majestic spectacle of swans in flight, as well as the more numerous geese. The largest bridge on the line,

BURE VALLEY RAILWAY

Length of line: *14.4km (9 miles)*
Operating periods: *Most days, Easter–October.*
Facilities: *Restaurant, shops, museum, model railway.*
Access for disabled:
  Special rolling stock for wheelchairs (advance notice appreciated); special toilets at Aylsham and Wroxham.
Public transport:
  Wroxham station, Eastern Counties buses from Norwich to Aylsham.
Nearby tourist attractions: *Blickling Hall (NT).*
Address:
  Aylsham Station, Norwich Road, Aylsham, Norfolk NR11 6BW.
Internet address: *http://www.bvrw.co.uk*
Telephone (information): *01263 733858*

32m (105 feet) long with three girder spans, takes the railway over the river as St Andrew's church tower at Buxton with Lamas can be seen over the tree tops to the right. The builder of the famous Euston Arch, Thomas Cubitt, was born here, and Anna Sewell, author of *Black Beauty*, lies buried in the Quaker Burial Ground.

Past the last loop at Brampton Halt and across more fields of beet, the line perceptibly dips to tunnel under the Norwich–Cromer line before climbing up into the grand terminus at Aylsham. The overall-roofed station provides shelter for the rolling stock as well as passengers, and the well-equipped station building has a small museum and model railway. The workshops to the right can usually be visited.

CHURNET VALLEY RAILWAY

For those who associate the area around the Potteries with the scars of a post-Industrial Revolution landscape, the Churnet Valley Railway

(CVR) may come as a surprise. A 1900 *Guide to the High Peak* eulogized that 'there are few more charming valleys in the kingdom ... the line passes through a most picturesque and beautiful district, every few yards traversed revealing new charms.' Even allowing for a degree of hyperbole, the writer was justly describing what, astonishingly, remains a remarkably unspoilt stretch of countryside. This is almost entirely due to the fact that no motor road has been built along the valley from the CVR's headquarters at Cheddleton. The absence of traffic pollution and noise has allowed flora and fauna to thrive to such an extent that there is a natural history centre and a series of woodland trails near the current southern limit of CVR operations at Consall Forge.

The Churnet Valley line from North Rode to Uttoxeter was built by the North Staffordshire

➡ The proximity of railway and canal at Consall Forge on the Churnet Valley make it a delightful setting for photographs, as here with LMS 0-6-0 tank No 47383 (from the Severn Valley).

◆Express trains between Manchester and London once emerged from Cheddleton Tunnel, bored through sandstone near Leekbrook Junction. BR 2-6-4 tank No 80136 heads south.

Railway (NSR), known affectionately as the 'Knotty' after the county's emblem. The line was surveyed by George Parker Bidder, the famous 'calculating boy' from Moretonhampstead in Devon. As a child Bidder's powers of rapid computation were displayed at country fairs, and when he reached his teenage years he applied his skills to engineering. Built with double track, the line opened in 1849, and at one time carried London–Manchester expresses with the shortest journey time between the cities.

Various schemes to preserve different parts of the Churnet Valley line were put forward by several societies during the 1970s. Oakamoor and Leek were proposed as possible centres, but the latter was scuppered by an obtuse council. Eventually, after establishing a base at Cheddleton, the CVR was able to purchase 11.2km (7 miles) of line from Leekbrook to Oakamoor. The section between Cheddleton and Leekbrook was opened to passenger trains in 1996, followed by the section south to Consall in 1998.

Cheddleton station has a delightful setting, with the River Churnet and the Caldon Canal close by, and lovely walks along both. The station building itself was saved by the prompt action of parish

▲There were over 400 'Jinty' 0-6-0 tanks on the London Midland & Scottish Railway, which developed the design from Midland origins. No 47383 is seen near Consall Forge.

CHURNET VALLEY RAILWAY

Length of line: *5.2km (3¼ miles)*
Operating periods: *Weekends throughout the year.*
Facilities: *Buffet, shop, museum.*
Access for disabled:
 Access to most of Cheddleton site, on trains by arrangement.
Public transport:
 Bus to Cheddleton village from Hamley, Longton and Leek.
Nearby tourist attractions:
 Cheddleton Flint Mill, Alton Towers.
Address:
 The Railway Station, Cheddleton, Staffordshire ST13 7EE.
Telephone (information): *01538 360522*

councillor Norman Hancock in 1974. Seeing the demolition squad about to start work, he persuaded them to allow a stay of execution. The poet laureate John Betjeman was one of many who helped to get the station listed. The Knotty set high standards at many of its stations, and several of those along the Churnet Valley were in the Tudor style it favoured. The station at Cheddleton was designed by William Sugden, though a board at the station goes so far as to suggest Augustus Pugin. In the welcoming tea room there is a fine cast-iron range and walls decorated with old photographs of Knotty stations – one is a view of Pipe Gate station in Edwardian times, with a window box running the full length of the signal box.

Notable in the station's small museum is one of the distinctive NSR signalman's chairs that had solid wings up the side to screen him from draughts. After a collision at Stoke station they were removed from main line signal boxes in 1872 on the recommendation of Lt Col F H Rich, who investigated the accident: 'These signalmen are on duty 12 hours, but I submit that it is not desirable that such comfortable means should be provided for the men to go to sleep while on duty and I recommend that the chairs should be removed at once from the signal cabins.'

Trains are propelled out of Cheddleton station because there is no means of running round the train on the now single line. The train weaves through hilly countryside and through the partly lined Cheddleton Tunnel (485m/531 yards) to reach the single platform at Leekbrook. There is no public access here and the boundary of the CVR is a

➤ Close to the Colne Valley Railway is the magnificent Norman tower of Hedingham Castle, begun in the late 11th or early 12th century. At 22.2m (73ft) high, it towers over the trees.

level-crossing, on the other side of which is the freight-only line leading to Caldon Low quarry.

The train returns and proceeds non-stop through Cheddleton, passing on the left the three-road engine shed that has been built on the site of the old goods yard.

The character of the valley becomes delightfully remote in the absence of any road and associated development or wires. On the left, craggy sandstone outcrops tower over the line, with bracken-covered slopes above. A small stone viaduct takes the railway over marshy ground on the floodplain of the Churnet, which is a blaze of marsh marigolds in the spring.

By the time the train draws into Consall, the valley has narrowed into a wooded defile in which there is room for little more than the railway, river and canal. In fact there is so little space that Consall southbound platform had a waiting shelter cantilevered out over the canal so that boats had to pass underneath it. The marvellous atmosphere of this lonely spot is helped by the antiquity of the few old cottages, the stationmaster's house and the Red Lion pub. Beside the canal wharf

are the remains of a few kilns. The nature centre is only 20 minutes' walk from Consall Forge.

Amongst the CVR's locomotives is one of the two surviving NSR locomotives, an 0-6-2 tank, and the very unusual NSR battery locomotive that once worked in the sidings that served the now-vanished copper works at Oakamoor, to which the CVR will one day run.

COLNE VALLEY RAILWAY

What this centre lacks in length of run, it makes up for in the presentation of exhibits, which extract the maximum educational and entertainment value. The project began in 1972, with the search for a home for an ex-War Department saddle tank, and developed into the reconstruction of 1.6km (1 mile) of railway along the trackbed of the Colne Valley & Halstead Railway. This was opened in 1860–3, and despite being put in the hands of the Official Receiver in 1874, passenger services survived until 1962.

Access to the 1.6km (1 mile) of trackbed was secured in 1973 and work began to create the Colne Valley Railway (CVR). The station from Sible & Castle

How things used to be on the Foxfield Steam Railway, until such enjoyable practices were deemed to be unsafe. Volcanic smoke effects and a noise to match were guaranteed.

Hedingham was generously given by its owner, dismantled and re-erected 3.2km (2 miles) away. The site now has two 61m (200ft) platforms, buildings housing a museum, café, shop and offices, and a signal box.

For such a modest line, the CVR has an astonishing collection of locomotives and rolling stock, including three main line locomotives: a Southern Railway Bulleid Pacific and two London Midland & Scottish Railway Black Five 4-6-0s.

FOXFIELD STEAM RAILWAY

The combined powers of the JCB and nature have often obliterated all trace of an industrial site. It would take a keen eye to detect that this railway is

COLNE VALLEY RAILWAY

Length of line: *1.6km (1 mile)*
Operating periods:
Sundays in late March–late October;
Tuesdays to Thursdays in summer school holidays.
Facilities: *Buffet, shop, picnic area, video carriage.*
Access for disabled:
Access to most areas, ramp for trains, no toilets.
Public transport:
Buses from Colchester, Braintree and Sudbury.
Nearby tourist attractions: *Castle Hedingham.*
Address:
Castle Hedingham Station, Yeldham Road,
Castle Hedingham, Halstead,
Essex CO9 3DZ.
Internet address: *http://www.ourworld.com/*
Telephone (information): *01787 461174*

◆ *The spectacle of the climb up the bank from Foxfield Colliery to Dilhorne is still enacted on special days, giving visitors a wonderful impression of the rural colliery railway.*

FOXFIELD STEAM RAILWAY

Length of line: *4.4km (2¼ miles)*
Operating periods:
   Sundays and Bank Holidays, April–September.
Facilities: *Buffet, shop.*
Access for disabled: *Access to most facilities.*
Public transport: *Blythe Bridge station.*
Nearby tourist attractions: *Trentham Gardens.*
Address:
   Foxfield Steam Railway, Blythe Bridge,
   Stoke-on-Trent.
Telephone (information): *01270 396210*

based on the branch built off the Stoke-on-Trent–Derby line in 1893 to serve a colliery. Coal was extracted at Foxfield from the 17th century until the pit closed in 1965. Usually that has been the end of the story – the site and trackbed erased faster than the memories of the men for whom it had been the focus of their working lives.

However, at Foxfield the site was taken over by a coal-processing and distributing company that numbered a few railway enthusiasts among its managers. With their help, the Foxfield Light Railway Society (FLRS) came into being to preserve the railway and operate the line with industrial tank engines. At first, passengers were taken in open trucks up the formidable 1 in 25 gradient out of the colliery site up to Dilhorne, accompanied by a magnificent sound from the tiny tank engine. But Health & Safety legislation put a stop to that fun, and today the line is more conventionally operated with proper coaches from proper platforms. Dilhorne, rather than the colliery, is also the terminus for trains from the main station at Caverswall Road, because it is not owned by the FLRS. None the less, occasional demonstration freight trains climbing up the bank recall the stirring sights and sounds of days gone by.

The FLRS station at Caverswall Road near Blythe Bridge station even has a North Staffordshire Railway signal box recovered from Hockley Crossing, as well as the usual amenities and workshops. The journey is surprisingly scenic, reminding passengers that many collieries had pleasant rural settings. The Staffordshire moors are a backdrop to woods and fields of grazing cows or corn, and many trains even have a bar and observation car from which to enjoy panoramic views.

GREAT CENTRAL RAILWAY

Almost every heritage railway is single track, whether it is based on a former double track main line or a quiet branch line that was always a single line. The Great Central Railway (GCR) is different: from the very beginning, the plan was to recreate the atmosphere and experience of a main line on which visitors could enjoy the spectacle of steam trains passing at speed.

The site chosen to bring that plan into fruition was particularly suitable, because the Great Central main

➥*Great Central main line express in the 1920s: one of Robinson's Class C4 4-4-2s built in 1903–6, No 6091, heads south from Rugby with a Newcastle–Bournemouth express.*

GREAT CENTRAL RAILWAY

Length of line: *12.8km (8 miles)*

Operating periods:
Weekends throughout the year, daily mid-May–late September.

Facilities: *Buffet, shop, museum, depot.*

Access for disabled:
Advance notice required for access at Loughborough; good access at Quorn and Rothley; special coach for wheelchairs (advance notice required); ramps at all stations.

Public transport:
Loughborough station, linking bus service.

Nearby tourist attractions:
Leicester: Belgrave Hall, Abbey Pumping Station; Quorn & Woodhouse: Bradgate Park, Whatoff Lodge; Loughborough: John Taylor Bell Foundry Museum.

Address:
*Loughborough Central Station,
Great Central Road, Loughborough,
Leicestershire LE11 1RW.*

Telephone (information): *01509 230726*

◆The GCR is the perfect railway for recreating main line scenes from the past. This picture of a grimy BR Class 9F, No 92203, at Kinchley Lane might have been taken pre-1968.

line between Nottingham and London Marylebone was the last main line into the capital and the last really important addition to the railway network. It owed its existence to the determination of one of Victorian Britain's greatest railway magnates, Sir Edward Watkin, who saw the GC main line forming a key part in a railway that would take trains from northern England to France through a tunnel under the English Channel. Consequently it was built for high speeds with relatively easy gradients and, most importantly, a loading gauge that matched the large size of continental carriages and wagons.

With characteristic lack of foresight, this exceptional national asset was discarded during the 1960s: freights were re-routed in 1965, the last semi-fast trains to London ceased in 1966 and the

◆A sense of the atmosphere that can be created at a major station like Loughborough Central station, especially at night, is given by this shot of LMS Pacific No 46229 **Duchess of Hamilton.**

GWR No 7029 **Clun Castle** *heads an 'up' express as No 44767 toils slowly northbound on a down mixed freight near Swithland, April 1994.*

remaining Rugby–Nottingham local service was withdrawn in 1969. A society named the Main Line Steam Trust was formed to preserve part of the line and took a lease of the offices at Loughborough station in 1970.

Since then, as the GCR, the society has rebuilt 12.8km (8 miles) of railway, much of it from bare trackbed – though thankfully all the stations except Belgrave & Birstall at the southern end were in a remarkably complete state. This has enabled the GCR to restore them as some of the finest stations in preservation, including such unusual items as a goods office at a wayside station. The largest project has been the restoration of 8.4km (5¼ miles) of double track between Rothley and Loughborough, and it is anticipated that this will be opened in the summer of 2000.

Most journeys start at the GCR's headquarters at Loughborough, where the station is laid out as an island platform like most of the stations on the GC main line. The wood-panelled booking hall at street level is linked to the platform by a covered staircase – the sole disadvantage of this type of station, which saved on the duplication of facilities implicit in a two-platform arrangement. The long platform at Loughborough has the largest glass canopy in railway preservation, a feature that has doubtless helped to attract film and television companies in search of the atmosphere of a bigger station. *Shadowlands* and *Goodnight Mr Tom* are just two of the recent productions shot at the station.

A cinder path – itself a rarity, and enough to conjure up highly nostalgic memories for those who visited engine sheds in the days of steam – takes visitors from the north end of the platform to the signal box and engine shed. Visitors are normally welcome to look around both, but a word with the signalman first is appreciated. The workshop of any well-equipped railway gives an idea of the scale of work required to maintain steam locomotives in service, as well as the special machine tools and other tackle needed to do the job.

The GCR passes through gently rolling pastoral countryside – ideal terrain for the Quorn hunt, which takes its name from the village served by the first station, Quorn & Woodhouse. The goods yard here was transformed by new sidings during the Second World War, so it was decided to present the station as it might have looked at the time, with a 'NAAFI' canteen and an air-raid shelter under the stairs. There is also a well-restored signal box and a model railway in a carriage in the goods yard.

Swithland Reservoir is the scenic high point of the journey and must be one of the most attractive municipal reservoirs in the country. Built to provide water for Leicester, it had to be drained while the brick and girder viaduct carrying the GC across it was built. Today the reservoir is home to thousands of birds, which are attracted by the trees of the surrounding Charnwood Forest.

Just south of the water there is a bridge over the road that leads from Swithland to Mountsorrel, where the quarries were linked to the GC by a short branch from Swithland Sidings. This area is another of the GCR's major projects: a pair of goods loops and the associated sidings have been reinstated to recreate a once common feature of main lines – the junction of an industrial branch line. The sidings are being put to appropriate use to stable the GCR's extensive collection of goods vehicles, which are periodically used for the revenue-earning photographers' specials, faithfully recreating scenes of bygone years.

In contrast to Quorn & Woodhouse, the station at Rothley has been restored to its Edwardian appearance as a smart intermediate station on the Great Central. It is worth pausing here, especially at dusk, to savour the atmosphere of a gas-lit station with superbly restored waiting room and goods office. Opposite the platform is the signal box, retrieved from Blind Lane at Wembley to replace the long-demolished original.

On the east side of the line, the GCR's carriage and wagon workshops can be seen as the train leaves the station. A deep cutting precedes an overbridge, which once afforded access to the vanished station at Belgrave & Birstall, a short distance north of the GCR's southern terminus at Leicester North. The facilities are rudimentary in comparison with the other stations because there are plans to create an imposing terminal station here when funds permit.

Another long-term scheme is to extend the GCR north to join up with an affiliated group relaying the line south along the trackbed from a country park at Ruddington. The greatest obstacle is the Midland main line to the north of the GCR station at Loughborough, which would have to be spanned by a costly bridge.

The GCR has over 20 locomotives based on the line, with examples of each of the four pre-nationalization companies' designs, though some are leased out to other railways just as the GCR hires them in.

MID-NORFOLK RAILWAY

The Great Eastern Railway (GER) network of branch lines that threaded its way across the heaths, woods and fertile farms of East Anglia was one of the most extensive and characterful of any of the

➤ *Before the axe was taken to most of East Anglia's cross-country lines, D16/3 4-4-0 No 62540 joins the Thetford–Norwich line at Wymondham with a train from East Dereham.*

pre-grouping railways. Many were lengthy cross-country routes, punctuated by remote, peaceful junctions that sprang to life a dozen times a day as two or three trains met to exchange passengers, parcels and local gossip. Few were more isolated than County School in Norfolk, which probably sees more weekend activity now than it ever did, even when the public school it served was thriving.

The school and all but its chapel have long gone but the railway is coming back to life, County School being the northern limit of the Mid-Norfolk Railway (MNR), one of the most recent additions to the ranks of heritage railways. It is an ambitious scheme and would not have come into being but for the vision of Breckland District Council, which bought the 17.6km (11 miles) between Wymondham and East Dereham and has leased the railway to the MNR for 99 years.

South Norfolk District Council and Norfolk County Council have also been staunch supporters, reflecting the awareness of progressive councils of the need to foster promising public transport and rail freight links. Their foresight has already been rewarded by a unique situation in which freight trains have returned to a heritage railway in advance of regular

➤Founded in the 12th century, Wymondham Abbey has two huge bell towers, one of octagonal form built by the monks and the other built to a square plan by the parishioners.

passenger services. Trains of Ministry of Defence traffic to and from places as far afield as Pembroke Dock and Tees Dock have taken hundreds of lorries off the area's roads. Operated by English Welsh & Scottish Railway, the trains have travelled over the branch to East Dereham, bringing welcome revenue to help the MNR to fulfil its objective of operating a passenger service for local people and tourists alike.

This includes reinstating a missing 1.6km (1 mile) of track north of East Dereham to reunite the main section with the County School outpost, to give a 27.2-km (17-mile) line. It is hoped that in the fullness of time, it may be possible to reopen the next 8km (5 miles) north to the town of Fakenham, the largest Norfolk town without a rail connection; this would pass one of the largest maltings in the county, offering the prospect of additional freight traffic. If this extension was achieved, it would create the longest preserved railway in Britain, at 35.2km (22 miles), eclipsing the West Somerset Railway by 3.2km (2 miles).

The railway reached Dereham, as it was then known, in 1847 and was extended on through County School to Fakenham the following year. It is indicative of the importance of these cross-country lines and the volume of traffic they once carried that the GER employed about 90 staff at Dereham, which had four signal boxes, an engine and goods shed, and a four-

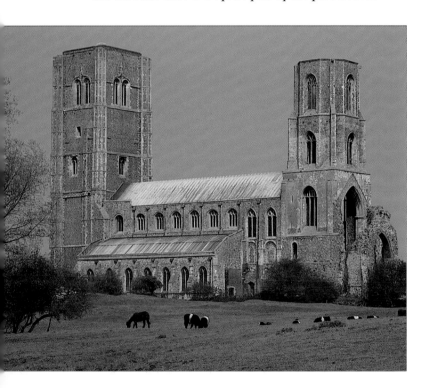

MID-NORFOLK RAILWAY

Length of line: *17.6km (11 miles)*
Operating periods:
  Reopening imminent – telephone for details.
Facilities: *Buffet, shop.*
Access for disabled:
  Ramp for access to trains; special toilet at Dereham.
Public transport:
  Wymondham station; buses X94, 55, 57 from Norwich to Dereham.
Nearby tourist attractions:
  Wymondham Abbey, Norfolk Rural Life Museum.
Address:
  The Railway Station, Station Road, Dereham, Norfolk NR19 1DF.
Telephone (information): *01362 690633*

platform station with refreshment room. A road-oriented transport policy steadily eroded traffic: passenger services north of Dereham to Wells ended in 1964, between Dereham and King's Lynn in 1968, and finally the link with the main Norwich–London line at Wymondham went in 1969. Freight survived for another 20 years, while an energetic local campaign gathered pace, pressing for the restoration of passenger services in some shape or form.

For the visitor, the attractive towns of Wymondham and Dereham have much to offer, and an excellent leaflet describes waymarked paths from County School station, through delightful countryside.

MIDLAND RAILWAY CENTRE

The Midland Railway (MR) was one of the great pre-grouping railway companies, which grew from the amalgamation of three Midlands-based companies in 1844 to become a national concern with a part share in the Forth Bridge. The Midland Railway Centre (MRC), which is devoted to preserving artefacts from its past, is situated in an incomparable

◆ The western end of the Midland Railway Centre's line crosses Butterley reservoir on a major earthwork. LMS 3F 0-6-0 tank No 47327 crosses with a Santa special.

setting in the East Midlands, appropriately connected to the former MR line of Railtrack between Leicester and Sheffield.

What sets the MRC apart from other heritage railways is the sheer scale of its principal site: the museum site at Swanwick Junction covers 23 hectares (57 acres), while adjacent to it is a rail-connected country park of 14 hectares (35 acres) and a farm museum. The idea for a commemoration of the MR came from Derby Borough Museums in 1969, but local government reorganization led to it being dropped. The volunteers who had become involved with the proposal offered to develop it, forming the Midland Railway Trust (MRT), which administers the MRC.

The MRC has been created on part of the MR opened in 1875 between Pye Bridge and Ambergate (Crich Junction), with a single intermediate station at Butterley, home of the famous ironworks that

produced the spans of the roof at St Pancras and numerous other great stations around the world. This cut-off was built primarily to relieve the congested Ambergate–Derby–Trent line of freight traffic coming from the Americas via Liverpool, enabling it to be routed down the Erewash Valley line. The line closed in 1968 and was truncated to the west of Butterley by reconstruction of the A38 at the site of Hammersmith Junction, where a branch went south to Derby through Ripley and Denby.

This left a 5.6-km (3½-mile) run between Hammersmith and Riddings Junction/Pye Bridge for the MRT to rebuild when it took over the line in 1973. With local authority help, the MRC has grown into a major attraction offering a wide range of activities. All visits have to begin at Butterley. Having lost its passenger services as long ago as 1930, the station here had completely disappeared when the MRT arrived. The handsome stone station seen today came from the MR station at Whitwell in north Derbyshire. A carriage and wagon repair works occupies the goods yard, which is signalled by the signal box from Ais Gill on the famous Settle & Carlisle line.

Heading east towards Pye Bridge, trains emerge from a deep cutting with the expanse of the Swanwick Junction site on the right, overlooked by the imposing, large signal box recovered from Kettering and nearby gantry from Shipley. Also on the right is the line to Butterley Ironworks. Remaining on the train, you will see on the left-hand side the restored Swanwick spur, which went off to a colliery. Beyond the museum site is the Country Park and the Jessop Monument, erected to commemorate William Jessop, who built the adjacent Cromford Canal and became one of the founders of the Butterley Company in 1790–1.

At the eastern terminus, within sight of the Midland main line, the engine runs round the train for the return to Butterley and the section on to Hammmersmith. Passengers are advised to alight at Swanwick Junction on this leg of the journey if they wish to see the museum, country park or farm. A path from the station leads to the demonstration signal box

◀ *One of the pleasures of a visit to the MRC is the splendid collection of Midland Railway signal boxes and signals. LMS 8F 2-8-0 No 48151 passes a fine bracket signal and box.*

One of the MRC's two BR 4MT 2-6-4 tanks waits to leave Butterley station for Swanwick Junction, with the signal box recovered from Ais Gill on the Settle–Carlisle line.

from Linby, north of Nottingham (now named Brands Crossing), in which visitors can learn the basics of railway signalling. Adjacent to the box is Brands Sidings station on the narrow gauge line that continues into the country park and passes near the mouth of Butterley canal tunnel (2840m/2966yd) on its way to Golden Valley.

The museum site offers a buffet, shop, a 'tin tabernacle 'Victorian church, road vehicle museum, the Matthew Kirtley Museum housing a wide variety of locomotives and rolling stock dating from the 1860s to the present, the Static Power Display of both steam and internal combustion engines, and a miniature railway. Beyond the gatehouse (from St Mary's goods yard in Derby) is Brittain Pit Farm Museum with a variety of animals.

Returning from Swanwick Junction, trains run through Butterley station non-stop to reach the western terminus at Hammersmith, where there is a small country station and signal box (from Kilby Bridge near Leicester). After running round the engine takes the train back to Butterley.

Most of the MRC's locomotives are of ex-MR or London Midland & Scottish Railway origin, the most historic being the lovely 2-4-0 designed by Matthew Kirtley and built in 1866. There is also one of the largest collections of retired main line diesel locomotives in the country.

NATIONAL TRAMWAY MUSEUM

In comparison with heritage railways, there are few places in Britain to see vintage trams at work. Yet the National Tramway Museum (NTM) at Crich in Derbyshire must be one of the finest tram museums in the world. Not only does it have an outstanding

MIDLAND RAILWAY CENTRE

Length of line: *5.6km (3½ miles)*
Operating periods:
*Most Saturdays and Sundays throughout the year;
Wednesdays April–October; daily certain weeks
in summer.*
Facilities:
*Buffet, shop, museum, country park, miniature
railway, narrow gauge railway, model railways.*
Access for disabled:
Access to buffet and shop, special toilets and coach.
Public transport:
*Derby station and Trent buses 243 and 245 to
Centre; Alfreton & Mansfield station and Trent buses
242 and 243 to Centre.*
Nearby tourist attractions:
Crich Tramway, Denby Potteries.
Address:
*Butterley Station, Ripley,
Derbyshire DE5 3QZ.*
Telephone (information):
01773 747674/749788
Telephone (timetable): *01773 570140*

collection of over 70 trams drawn from places as far afield as Johannesburg, Prague and New York, but it is in a wonderful setting.

Situated at an improbably high level in the hills overlooking the picturesque Derwent Valley near Cromford, the NTM begins in a recreated Victorian street with some imposing façades as well as solid three-dimensional buildings housing such amenities as tea room, shop and museum. The museum provides a fascinating introduction to the best form of powered mechanical transport for urban areas – leaving the visitor bewildered at the folly of a nation that got rid of trams. Realizing what a mistake that decision was, in many areas they are now being put back in an effort to try to reduce urban pollution and congestion.

Perhaps the most evocative time to visit the NTM is in the autumn for one of the gas-lit events, when the soft yellow glow from the street lamps combines with the creamy electric lights from the trams to create a wonderfully atmospheric picture. It is best to arrive early, because it is a pity to miss the views over the valley during the 1.6-km (1-mile) journey along the hill.

☛ *The authentic re-creation of Victorian street scenes has been one of the triumphs of the National Tramway Museum, seen here with trams from Blackpool and Johannesburg.*

NATIONAL TRAMWAY MUSEUM

Length of line: *1.6km (1 mile)*
Operating periods:
 Daily April–October, except Fridays in May,
 September and October.
Facilities:
 Buffet, shop, video theatre, museum, tram depots,
 playground, picnic areas.
Access for disabled:
 Access to all facilities; specially adapted tram;
 trained staff; braille guide books.
Public transport:
 Bus from Matlock or Belper stations – telephone
 Busline on 01332 292200 for times.
Nearby tourist attractions:
 Cromford Mill, High Peak Trail,
 Peak District Mining Museum,
 Midland Railway Centre.
Address:
 Crich, Matlock,
 Derbyshire DE4 5DP.
Telephone (information): *01773 852565*

Among the trams is a rare example of a steam tram, built in 1885 by Beyer Peacock of Manchester for the New South Wales government but returned to Britain to become works shunter at Beyer Peacock.

NENE VALLEY RAILWAY

A seemingly disproportionate number of the clergy have had an interest in railways, ranging from the passing to the passionate. The Rev. Richard Paten was one of the latter, and it was his purchase of a British Rail steam locomotive in 1968 that provided the unwitting catalyst for the creation of the Nene Valley Railway (NVR). A former engineer, the Rev. Paten's intention had been to display 4-6-0 No 73050 on a plinth to commemorate Peterborough's links with the railways. The engine arrived under its own steam from

◆London County Council open-topped tram No 106 approaches the main terminus at the National Tramway Museum at Crich. Note the attention to detail in the street furniture.

Patricroft shed in Manchester, and it seemed a pity to 'stuff and mount' an engine in such good condition. Local volunteers helped to restore the locomotive and the Peterborough Locomotive Society (PLS) was formed.

In the early 1970s a proposal was made by the city and county councils to create a museum around Peterborough East station and use the Nene Valley line as a running track. When this came to nothing, the PLS called a meeting at the town hall and the idea of the NVR was taken up. Working with the councils and the Peterborough Development Corporation, the railway between Longueville and Yarwell junctions was bought and leased to the newly formed society.

Standing on Peterborough station today, only a few minutes' walk from the NVR station, it is hard to believe that the first railway into the city was not from the direction of either London or York. It came from the west, leaving the London & North Western Railway (LNWR) London–Birmingham line at Blisworth and proceeding to Peterborough via Northampton, Oundle and Wansford – the route of the NVR. The first train arrived in 1845, greeted by a crowd of over 8000 onlookers – 1000 more than Peterborough's population at the time – and there were four through trains a day to and from Euston. The last passenger services over the NVR section were withdrawn in 1966 and goods services ceased in 1972, two years before it was bought for preservation.

Although the track was still in situ, little else was – even the elegant Tudor-style station building at Wansford had been leased and the signal box had become a chicken coop. Reconstruction began, and further locomotives and rolling stock were acquired. Many of these were purchased from abroad, partly because of the dearth of easily restorable engines available by this time, and partly because there were no structures to preclude their operation on the NVR. This has been a commercial boon to the railway, since film companies wanting 'foreign-looking' trains did not have to travel abroad for them.

The NVR reopened in 1977 with a new eastern terminus at Orton Mere, adjacent to the 809-hectare (2000-acre) Nene Park, before the final extension, requiring long negotiations and much tracklaying, to Peterborough Nene Valley station in 1986. A link with Railtrack allows not only the exchange of stock or passenger trains, but also the occasional freight train.

NENE VALLEY RAILWAY

Length of line: *12km (7½ miles)*
Operating periods:
*Sunday January–October; Saturday April –October;
daily except Monday mid-July–August.*
Facilities: *Buffet, shop, museum, depot.*
Access for disabled:
*Access to stations and shop; special toilets at
Wansford; assistance boarding trains using ramps.*
Public transport: *Peterborough station.*
Nearby tourist attractions:
Elton Hall, Peterborough Cathedral.
Address:
*Wansford Station, Stibbington, Peterborough,
Cambridgeshire PE8 6LR.*
Telephone (information): *01780 784444*
Telephone (timetable): *01780 784440*

Passengers starting their journey at Peterborough can visit Railworld, an independent museum devoted to the world's railways, as well as looking at the NVR's collection of stock which, together with the station, stands on the site of the six-road LNWR engine sheds, closed in 1932 and demolished in 1965. Leaving Peterborough the train passes a signal box that once stood at Welland Bridge in Spalding. A line on the left soon comes into view: this is the link line with Railtrack, and the junction is controlled by the Midland Railway signal box at Orton Mere, which came from Helpston.

Orton Mere station has a passing loop for two-train operations, and all the land to the right is now part of the huge municipal country park created for the people of Peterborough. Its boating lakes,

➤*Bulleid unrebuilt Battle of Britain class Pacific No 34081*
92 Squadron *enters Wansford station past the fine LNWR signal box and highly inauthentic new station building.*

A photographers' special passes the signal box at Wansford with a recreated express goods. LNER A3 Pacific No 60103 Flying Scotsman has been given the alias of No 60039 Sandwich.

miniature railway and canoe course can also be reached from Ferry Meadows station, built on the site of Orton Waterville station, which closed in 1942. There follows a remarkably straight stretch of track of about 4.8km (3 miles) almost to Wansford.

Crossing the River Nene by Lynch Bridge, the train tackles the steepest gradient on the line at a modest 1 in 270, before passing the site of the Roman settlement of Durobrivae, which has produced treasures of such quality that they are now in the British Museum. Roman Castorware (the name of the village to the north) was widely exported and remnants have been found as far away as Turkey.

On the right just before another crossing of the river can be seen the trackbed of a line that went north to Stamford, which closed to passengers as long ago as 1929. Also on the right before the old Great

North Road level-crossing and station at Wansford is the splendid LNWR signal box of 1907. Wansford is the headquarters of the NVR and it is worth having a look around the engine shed at the cosmopolitan collection of locomotives from Sweden, Denmark, Germany and France.

Continuing west, the line burrows under the A1 before plunging into Wansford Tunnel, its decorative portal built with stone blocks that once held the rails of the London & Birmingham Railway before wooden sleepers were devised. The train slows and stops on an embankment at the site of Yarwell

169

NORTH NORFOLK RAILWAY

Length of line: *8.4km (5¼ miles)*

Operating periods:

Daily June–September except Mondays in June; Sundays March, April and October and holiday weeks.

Facilities: *Buffet, shops, museum, depot.*

Access for disabled:

Specially adapted Pullman car.

Public transport: *Sheringham station.*

Nearby tourist attractions:

Felbrigg Hall (NT), Sheringham Park (NT), Norfolk Coast Path.

Address:

Sheringham Station, Sheringham, Norfolk NR26 8RA.

Telephone (information): *01263 822045*

Telephone (timetable): *01263 825449*

Junction, where the lines from Northampton and Rugby met. A loop allows the engine to run round the train before returning to Peterborough.

NORTH NORFOLK RAILWAY

Of the many cross-country lines that ambled across Norfolk, one was built primarily for tourist traffic – the section of what became the Midland & Great Northern Joint (M&GN) between Melton Constable and Cromer was opened in 1887. The tourist potential of the area was promoted by a Victorian journalist and poet named Clement Scott, who dubbed the area 'Poppyland', a name that endured after the memory of its author had faded.

After the grouping of 1922, the M&GN became the joint property of the London Midland & Scottish

➤ *During dry weather diesel locomotives have to haul trains over the section of the North Norfolk Railway between Weybourne and Holt, where Class 27 D5386 runs round.*

and London & North Eastern railways until, in 1936, control passed into the hands of the latter. It was not vigorously promoted, and the reliance on holiday excursion traffic did not produce a healthy balance sheet. Almost all 293km (183 miles) of the line were closed to passengers in 1959, freight lingering on short stretches into the 1970s. The line from Sheringham to Melton Constable lasted until 1964. The only passenger section that survives today is that between Cromer and Sheringham, operated by Anglia Railways.

As soon as closure was mooted in the late 1950s, the M&GN Joint Preservation Society (M&GNRPS) was formed, making it one of the oldest in Britain. It took five years for its objectives to focus on the Sheringham to Weybourne section, which was purchased on closure in 1964, though not before demolition contractors had lifted all the track and sidings at Weybourne.

British Rail used the station at Sheringham until 1967, when a new halt on the other side of a level-crossing was built. This released the fine station for occupation by the M&GNRPS, which became the North Norfolk Railway (NNR) in 1976, a year after reopening to the public. In 1989, the NNR was extended beyond Weybourne to the market town of Holt.

There is plenty to see at Sheringham before catching the train. On platform 2 is a W H Smith bookstall that once stood at London Waterloo. It is on loan from the National Railway Museum and is now devoted to a model railway exhibition and sales. A LNER coach beside platform 2 contains an interesting collection of M&GN memorabilia and photographs, conveying something of its history and appeal. Many

➡ Weybourne station looking east in 1973 before work on restoring the station began. The large station was built in 1900 in expectation of substantial holiday traffic.

visitors enjoy trying their hand at pulling signal levers in the former East box, moved away from its site beside the level-crossing and now used for demonstrations. The operational signal box is built on the site of Sheringham West box, using the structure relocated from Wensum Junction in Norwich and the Great Eastern Railway lever frame from Loughton in Essex, the last mechanical signal box on the London Underground.

The NNR crosses land designated an Area of Outstanding Natural Beauty to reach Weybourne, and it is not hard to see why it has been protected. The line climbs steadily on a 1 in 92 gradient that taxes the smaller engines, with views of the sea to the north and wooded hills to the south. The woods are part of the National Trust's Sheringham Park estate, with parkland

☛ Close to the National Trust house of Felbrigg Hall is the late 14th-century St Margaret's church, once surrounded by the village of Felbrigg. The church still has its Georgian box pews.

landscaped by Humphry Repton. The gradient stiffens to 1 in 80 before the engine can shut off for Weybourne station.

Although the fine and commodious station buildings of 1900 survive, many of the other components had to be imported and have eclectic origins. The footbridge came from Stowmarket and the signal box from Holt, transferred in 1967 before there was any thought of extending the line westwards. The goods yard is the NNR's locomotive headquarters, with an engine shed that once stood at Norwich City station, which was the M&GN terminus. A purpose-built machine shop has been added. There is direct access to the Kelling Heath Nature Trail from the station platform.

The heathland between Weybourne and Holt is vulnerable to fire in the summer, so in dry periods the fire brigade ask the NNR to suspend steam haulage and use diesel power. The station at Holt is not on the site of the original, which was 1.6km (1 mile) to the south-west. It is worth breaking the journey to walk,

or take the horse bus that meets some trains, into the Georgian town of Holt.

Of the NNR's locomotive fleet, two stand out: LNER B12/3 4-6-0 No 8572 is the only surviving inside-cylindered 4-6-0 in Britain, and the Great Eastern J15 0-6-0 No 7564 of 1912 is also a unique survivor of a once numerous class.

PEAK RAIL

To travel from London to Scotland today, passengers have to choose either the West Coast route from Euston or the East Coast route from King's Cross. Until the 1960s it was also possible to travel from St Pancras, and judging by what passed by the window this was without question the finest route. The *pièce de résistance* was the Settle & Carlisle line

◆Britain's only surviving inside-cylindered 4-6-0, LNER B12/3 No 8572, heads towards Weybourne. The engine was built by Beyer Peacock in Manchester in 1928 and was recently restored.

through the Pennines, but the stretch of line through the Peak District between Ambergate and Chinley was scarcely less spectacular.

The line was finally opened to through traffic in 1867 after protests from, amongst others, John Ruskin about putting a line through such places as Monsal Dale. It was the route of Anglo-Scottish expresses as well as local passenger trains and freight until the decision was taken to re-route them and close the line completely between Matlock and Peak Forest (to the east of Buxton) a century after it was opened.

PEAK RAIL

Length of line: *6.4km (4 miles)*
Operating periods:
Sundays throughout the year; Saturdays
April —October and December; irregular weekdays.
Facilities: *Buffet, shops.*
Access for disabled:
At Darley Dale and Rowsley, but not
Matlock Riverside.
Public transport: *Matlock station.*
Nearby tourist attractions:
Cromford Mill, National Tramway Museum,
Cauldwell's Mill (Rowsley).
Address:
Matlock Station, Matlock,
Derbyshire DE4 3NA.
Telephone (information): *01629 580381*

▶ *Rebuilt West Country Pacific No 34101* **Hartland** *passes the handsome stone buildings of Darley Dale station on the Peak Rail line between Matlock and Rowsley.*

In 1975 the Peak Railway Society (PRS) was formed to reopen the line and took a lease of the trackbed at Darley Dale. The PRS worked south to reopen the line to a new station at Matlock Riverside, reached by a footpath from the Central Trains station, and then rebuilt the line north to the current terminus at Rowsley South. The railway threads the valley of the River Derwent to its junction with the Wye, the beautiful hills of the south-eastern Peak District towering above.

The solid Gothic station buildings of 1872 at Darley Dale were designed by Joseph Glossop, the soot-stained stonework recalling that this area had its share of mills and chimneys. A fine Midland Railway signal box transferred from Bamford on the Hope Valley line stands by the level-crossing, controlling the gates and the loop that now allows locomotives to run round their trains. This is where the railway keeps its locomotives (predominantly diesel) and rolling stock.

At Rowsley South, a brick-built platform has been erected on the east side of the line. To the west, in a wood of birch trees that has grown up on the site, the footings of the four-road engine shed designed by the MR and completed in 1923 are being excavated and

▲BR Class 4MT No 75069 catches the evening sun near Foley Park with a fine rake of Great Western Railway coaches. This engine spent most of its life on the Southern Region.

the track reinstated. The plan is to erect a much-needed shed to cover the engines, and to build a carriage shed.

Beyond the buffer stops at Rowsley lies the trackbed of one of the most attractive sections of railway in Britain, which runs through the Peak District National Park. Now that 22 million largely car-borne visitors intrude upon the supposed peace of the Park, an increasing number of people are coming round to the view that the occasional train would be infinitely preferable to the incessant noise of traffic and its attendant pollution. So it may come to pass that trains will once again thread Monsal Dale, in an effort to restore some of the area's lost quiet and beauty.

◆ *GWR 2-6-0 No 7325 near Hampton Loade on a frosty February morning, operating a special charter for photographers. Such events are a welcome source of income out of season.*

SEVERN VALLEY RAILWAY

The Severn Valley Railway (SVR), at 26.4km (16½ miles), is one of Britain's longest heritage railways and it has some tremendous assets that have helped to maintain its buoyant passenger figures. It runs through one of the prettiest valleys in the West Midlands, with frequent views over Britain's longest river. The stations are so well cared for that in the case of Bridgnorth they are part of the town's 'Britain in Bloom' entry. There are real ale bars at each terminus, and for railway enthusiasts a large and varied collection of locomotives and rolling stock, coupled with the largest signal box on a steam railway.

The Severn Valley line was popular with the people of the West Midlands long before there was any need to 'preserve' railways. At weekends they took the train to one of the stations close to the river for a picnic, a

SEVERN VALLEY RAILWAY

Length of line: *26.4km (16½ miles)*
Operating periods:
  Every weekend; daily mid-May–early October.
Facilities:
  Buffet, shops, model railways, Kidderminster Railway Museum.
Access for disabled:
  Special toilets at Kidderminster and Bridgnorth; special coach by prior arrangement.
Public transport: *Kidderminster station.*
Nearby tourist attractions:
  West Midland Safari Park, Bewdley Museum, Hartlebury Castle, Dudmaston (NT).
Address:
  Railway Station, Bewdley, Worcestershire DY12 1BG.
Telephone (information): *01299 403816*
Telephone (timetable): *01299 401001*

◀ GWR 2-6-0 No 7325 leaves Hampton Loade with a charter train. The signal box here had to be rebuilt, but the station buildings were still standing when the SVR bought the line.

walk or a spot of fishing. The number of riverside pubs testifies to the volume of 'day-trippers', as they were known.

The railway by which they came was part of the Great Western Railway (GWR), the line running from Shrewsbury and Buildwas in the north to Bewdley in the south, where lines forked to Kidderminster and Hartlebury. It opened throughout in 1862, but was never a prosperous line, served by only four return passenger trains a day for much of its 101 years, supplemented by extra workings south of Bridgnorth and helped by coal traffic from pits around Highley.

After closure of most of the route in 1963, the track north of Bridgnorth was lifted, but passenger services to Bewdley and coal from Alveley Colliery lingered until 1969 and 1970 respectively. The Severn Valley Railway Society was formed in 1965, and the first public trains began between Bridgnorth and Hampton Loade in 1970. There was so little expectation of the SVR proceeding further south that the signal box at Arley was dismantled for re-erection at Hampton Loade, compelling the railway to import another signal box, from Yorton between Crewe and Shrewsbury, when Arley was reached in 1974.

Gradually the railway progressed further south, reaching the lovely riverside town of Bewdley and finally achieving the ultimate goal of linking up with British Rail in 1984, when an entirely new GWR-style terminus opened on the site of the goods yard at Kidderminster. The link at Kidderminster not only enables passengers to arrive easily by rail, but also enables the easy exchange of locomotives or rolling stock on loan to or from other railways. Excursion trains, too, can gain access to the SVR for a journey to Bridgnorth.

Before leaving Kidderminster it is worth spending some time in the independent, but affiliated, Kidderminster Railway Museum, which has a vast collection of railway memorabilia as well as hands-on exhibits. At the throat of the station is the largest signal box on a heritage railway, and on the left is the massive goods shed that served the carpet-producing town and now acts as the SVR's carriage works.

▲Bewdley in British Railways days: BR Class Class 3MT No 82005 waits to leave with a train for Shrewsbury. The scene has changed remarkably little thanks to the care of the SVR.

Beyond a bridge on the right is a large compound for rolling stock, where a much-needed carriage shed will be built when the money is available.

Curving to the right the SVR runs through the suburbs of Kidderminster, modern houses on the left covering the site of the GWR engine shed. Falling Sands Viaduct crosses over both the River Stour and the Staffordshire & Worcestershire Canal. Passing on the left, a sugar beet factory that used to generate substantial traffic for the railway, the line enters a deepening cutting before plunging into the 439m (480yd) Bewdley Tunnel. Emerging from the tunnel, the character of the line changes abruptly as it passes through heathland and then fields to reach Bewdley, heralded by the sight of wild animals in the safari park to the right.

Bewdley perfectly retains the character of the small market town junction, with two signal boxes, three platforms and generous siding accommodation, now full of rolling stock and locomotives under repair. Soon after leaving Bewdley by the eight-arch Wribbenhall Viaduct, which affords good views over the home town of Stanley Baldwin, the trackbed of the branch that once dropped down to cross the river on its way to Tenbury Wells and Woofferton Junction can be seen.

For the rest of the journey, the railway follows the Severn, though it is out of sight beyond Eardington. Other water in the shape of Trimpley Reservoir is passed on the left, before a steep-sided cutting leads on to the most spectacular crossing of the Severn by the majestic arch of Victoria Bridge, engineered by Sir John Fowler and cast by the famous Coalbrookdale

▶The west front of the National Trust House of Dudmaston overlooks the garden and artificial lake. The house was built in 1695–1701 for Sir Thomas Wolryche.

On the penultimate day of British Railways services, Ivatt 2-6-2 tank No 41207 waits to leave Bridgnorth for Kidderminster. The SVR engine shed now occupies the goods yard.

Company. The view along the river is as impressive as the view of the bridge from the riverside walk that can be reached from the next station at Arley. Like all SVR stations, Arley has been beautifully restored, with commendable attention to detail – such as replacing concrete sleepers with wood within the station limits, and adding the period luggage, station garden and enamel advertising signs that help to create the kind of atmosphere that draws film and television productions.

Another deep cutting precedes the single platform at Highley, where coal was brought to the railway from four pits in the adjacent hills, reaching the station by standard and narrow gauge lines, aerial ropeways and inclined planes. The sidings that served Alveley are passed before Hampton Loade, another popular spot

for fishermen. Woodland interrupts the passengers' view of the river as the train runs along the slope of a hill towards journey's end at Bridgnorth, where an historic footbridge links the station with the old part of the town.

The SVR's locomotive workshops are based at Bridgnorth, and include an impressive boiler shop that carries out contract work for other heritage railways. The locomotive fleet is appropriately dominated by GWR engines, but there are plenty of London Midland & Scottish Railway designs and a London & North Eastern Railway K4 2-6-0 that spent its early life amongst the scenic glories of the West Highland lines.

WELLS & WALSINGHAM LIGHT RAILWAY

Unlike most miniature railways, the Wells & Walsingham Light Railway (WLLR) provides a useful service, linking the seaside resort of Wells with the intriguing village of Little Walsingham. The WLLR also has the distinction of being the longest 260mm (10¼in) gauge railway in the world, at 6.4km (4 miles).

Opened in 1982, the railway uses the trackbed of the former Great Eastern Railway branch from Wells to County School, and most trains are hauled by an impressive 2-6-0+0-6-2 Garratt built by Neil Simkins in 1986.

Walsingham was renowned for its shrine, visited by many English kings, and the remains of the priory can be seen in the grounds of the modern abbey.

The 2-6-0+0-6-2 Garratt designed and built by Neil Simkins in 1986 leaves the station at Wells. The WLLR was the first 260mm (10¼in) gauge line to obtain a Light Railway Order.

WELLS & WALSINGHAM LIGHT RAILWAY

Length of line: *6.4km (4 miles)*
Operating periods: *Daily Easter–September.*
Facilities: *Buffet, shop.*
Access for disabled: *Limited.*
Public transport: *Eastern Counties bus.*
Nearby tourist attractions: *Thursford Collection, Shirehall Museum.*
Address: *Wells next the Sea, Norfolk NR23 1RB.*
Telephone (information): *01328 710631*

CHAPTER 5

NORTHERN ENGLAND & THE ISLE OF MAN

The north of England, particularly the north east, is the birthplace of railways. It was here that they played a vital role in Britain's transition to a fully industrialized society.

◀*The Groudle Glen Railway on the Isle of Man is a delightful narrow gauge line, with spectacular views and this lovely Bagnall 2-4-0, built in 1896, named* **Sea Lion**.

◀*No 12* **Hutchinson**, *seen here in Santon cutting, was built by Beyer Peacock in 1908 with medium boiler. It was chosen to haul the official 'last train' from Ramsey in 1968.*

BEAMISH (NORTH OF ENGLAND OPEN AIR MUSEUM)

This is one of the country's largest open air museums. Whole streets from towns and pit villages provide an astonishingly vivid insight into innumerable facets of life in the north-east of Victorian Britain. These are complemented by rural displays around Pockerley Manor and horse yard.

The railway naturally plays an important part in the 80.9-hectare (200-acre) site and focuses on the re-creation of a typical North Eastern Railway (NER) country terminus. The attractive stone station of 1867 came from Rowley to the west of Consett, the 1896 signal box came from Carr House East, also near Consett, and the large goods shed from Alnwick. The all-important weighbridge, which was used to place the right tariff on all goods traffic, was rescued from

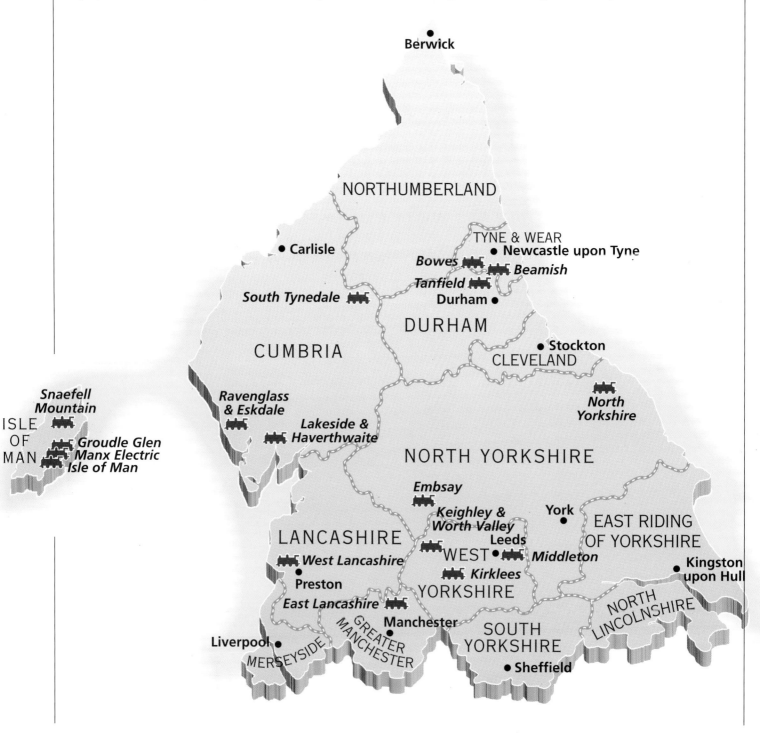

➤ There was never a railway on this site at Beamish, so everything has been rescued from elsewhere in the north east and re-erected to re-create a North Eastern Railway station.

Glanton in Northumberland and is at the entrance of the drive to the goods yard.

Besides some industrial engines, the museum has an appropriate NER C1 class 0-6-0, built at Gateshead in 1889 and restored in the pleasing lined apple green of the NER. It also has what is believed to be the third oldest steam engine in the world – the 1822 0-4-0 designed by George Stephenson for use at Hetton Colliery. Pre-grouping rolling stock is inevitably rare and is used by most heritage railways on special trains, but Beamish has a delightful composite (more than one class) clerestory coach of 1903, magnificently restored in the NER maroon livery that was used for a time.

There is also a tram line that negotiates part of the site, using a variety of tramcars drawn from various towns and cities in northern Britain.

BEAMISH (NORTH OF ENGLAND OPEN AIR MUSEUM)

Length of line: *0.8km (½mile)*
Operating periods: *Almost daily.*
Facilities: *Restaurant, tea room, shops.*
Access for disabled: *Limited.*
Public transport:
  Bus from Eldon Square, Newcastle; bus nos 775 and 778 from Sunderland; bus no 720 from Milburngate, Durham.
Nearby tourist attractions:
  Tanfield Railway, Gibside Chapel (NT).
Address:
  Beamish, County Durham
  DH9 0RG.
Telephone (information): *01207 231811*

BOWES RAILWAY

The word 'unique' is greatly over-used, but the Bowes Railway can be justly described as that. It is the only preserved cable incline in Britain, the last of a once-common method of hauling goods wagons and occasional passenger carriages up gradients too steep for adhesion working by steam locomotives. This was achieved by having a stationary steam engine at the summit of the incline, which hauled wagons up by means of a cable guided by rollers between the rails. A measure of the railway's historical importance is that English Heritage has given it the status of an Ancient Monument, which is exceptional for industrial remains.

On arrival, visitors are given an introduction to this extraordinary railway, which was built in the 1820s to take coal from a network of collieries to staithes on the River Tyne at Jarrow. The 24-km (15-mile) line had seven rope-worked inclines, linked by steam-

---

BOWES RAILWAY

Length of line: *2km (1¼ miles)*
Operating periods:
Second and fourth Sundays in the month;
Easter–September.
Facilities: *Buffet, shop, guided tours.*
Access for disabled:
Special toilet and access to refreshment room.
Public transport:
Buses 187 and 188 from Gateshead Metro.
Nearby tourist attractions:
Beamish, Tanfield Railway.
Location: *Springwell Village, near Gateshead.*
Telephone (information): *0191 416 1847*

☛ *The skilled task of removing the rope from the path of the moving wagons is one of the principal sights at the Bowes Railway, the last remaining rope-worked incline in Britain.*

hauled sections, but falling demand for coal led to closure in 1974.

Thanks to the initiative of Tyne & Wear County Council, the entire route was not lifted for scrap, or the buildings razed. The Council bought the 2-km (1¼-mile) section between Black Fell, at the foot of the incline from Blackham's Hill, and a main yard at Springwell. After a tour of the buildings at Springwell, visitors then have the novel experience of a ride in a steam-hauled converted brake van to the winding house at Blackham's Hill. Sadly the steam engine that once powered the incline was replaced

in 1950 by a Metropolitan Vickers electric hauler.

The real drama of the incline takes place outside, as a rake of wooden-bodied wagons is hauled up the gradient, which varies between 1 in 18 and 1 in 37. As the wagons approach the summit, two men have the skilful task of dragging the rope out of the path of the moving wagons as soon as it is released from the leading wagon by a special coupling.

*On loan to the Bowes Railway from British Gypsum, Barclay 0-4-0 saddle tank **W.S.T.** was built in 1954 and spent most of its life at Cocklakes works to the south of Carlisle.*

▲LMS Class 5 4-6-0 No 5407 leaves Irwell with a train from Rawtenstall to Bury. Eighteen of Stanier's Class 5s have been saved and are ideal locomotives for longer lines.

Appropriately, the locomotive fleet is composed entirely of industrial steam and diesel engines, and there is a large collection of open wagons to give a feeling of authenticity to the sidings area at Springwell.

EAST LANCASHIRE RAILWAY

For over a century, Britain's industrial areas were criss-crossed by dense networks of lines that served every colliery, factory and quarry of any size, each junction requiring its own signal box or ground frame to control the points and signals. Typical of these lines was the Bury to Rawtenstall section of the East Lancashire Railway (ELR), the title of which has been revived for the heritage railway that first reopened to passengers in 1987.

All along the route, which first opened in 1846, sidings went off to serve mills and factories, vital conduits of trade when Britain was the world's foremost manufacturing nation. Today those links are gone, as have most of the buildings they served. Even those that remain are seldom fulfilling their original function.

Nature has reasserted itself along much of the Irwell Valley followed by the ELR, and the scenery is a pleasant surprise for many passengers. The vibrant valley communities also make the ELR's intermediate stations useful starting points for walks or visits to the many local events, ranging from music festivals to agricultural fairs. The tourist potential was certainly an important factor when the Greater Manchester Council and various other councils decided to support the ELR's objectives by contributing to the line's purchase.

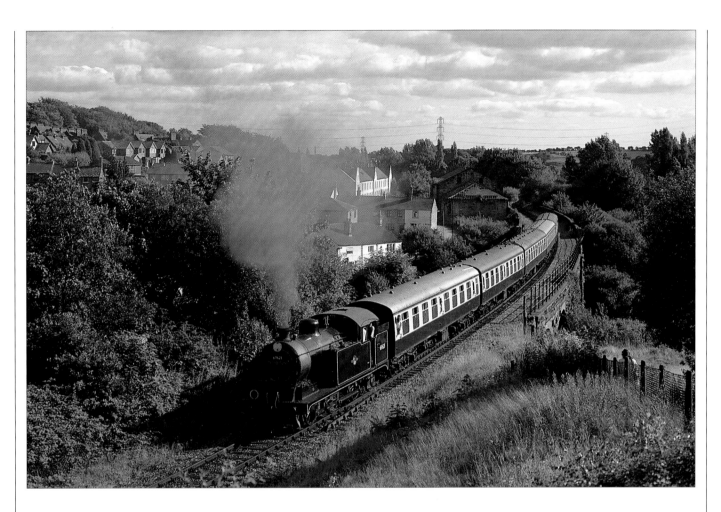

On loan from the East Anglian Railway Museum, LNER N7/4 0-6-2 tank No 69621 crosses Brooksbottom Viaduct en route to Rawtenstall. The coaches are in early BR livery.

The easiest way to reach the ELR is by Metrolink to Bury Interchange, only a short walk from the ELR Bolton Street station. Although this is one of the largest stations on a heritage railway, there is a bland 1950s structure on the site of its fire-damaged predecessor, though this may be replaced one day. The line enters a short tunnel that was given an attractive northern portal to commemorate the remains of Bury's medieval castle, which were excavated during the tunnel's construction. On the left is the ELR's engine shed (its workshops are to the south of Bolton Street station).

The line soon enters open country and an area strongly associated with the Peel family, whose wealth generated by local cotton mills allowed (Sir) Robert Peel to go into politics and eventually become prime minister. During his period as home secretary, he reorganized the London police force – hence the

EAST LANCASHIRE RAILWAY

Length of line: *12.8/19.2km (8/12 miles)*
Operating periods:
Saturdays, Sundays and Bank Holidays throughout the year.
Facilities:
Buffet, shop, museum.
Access for disabled:
Special toilets at Bury, Ramsbottom and Rawtenstall; special coach for disabled (please telephone in advance).
Public transport:
Bury railway and Metrolink stations.
Nearby tourist attractions:
Helmshore Textile Museum.
Address:
Bolton Street Station, Bury, Lancashire BL9 0EY.
Telephone (information): *0161 764 7790*

◀*GWR 2-8-0 tank No 5224, on loan from the Great Central Railway, and LMS 4F 0-6-0 No 4422, borrowed from the Churnet Valley Railway, at Ramsbottom station.*

names 'Peelers' and 'Bobbies'. Peel Mill still stands near the site of Tottington Junction, where the branch to Holcombe Brook went off to the west; this was once electrified at the unusual voltage of 3600V using overhead wires.

The first of many crossings of the Irwell precedes the first station at Summerseat, a pleasant village where the impressive pile of Hoyle's Mill has been converted into apartments and a pub/restaurant. A path leads around the back of the mill to the hidden gem of Gollinrod Gorge. Leaving Summerseat, the line crosses the 182-m (200-yd) Brooksbottom Viaduct overlooking Hoyle's Mill on the right and plunges into Brooksbottom Tunnel, bored through solid rock, followed by Nuttall Tunnel. The northern portal is decorated with carved faces, reputedly of the original ELR's directors.

The Irwell is crossed by two more bridges before arrival at Ramsbottom, an unspoilt town with a heritage trail that capitalizes on the connections with Dickens: much of the town was built by the Grant brothers of Nuttall Hall, who were the models for the Cheeryble brothers in *Nicholas Nickelby*.

North of Ramsbottom is the site of Stubbins Junction, where the old ELR main line proceeded north to Accrington, while the Bacup line that forms the route of today's ELR bears to the east towards the new station at Irwell Vale. This has been created by the ELR to encourage exploration of the surrounding countryside, which includes Stubbins Nature Reserve and Helmshore Textile Museum. It also affords access to the largest concentrated public arts project in the country – the Irwell Sculpture Trail.

The valley opens out again and the site of Ewood Bridge station is passed with little left to indicate that there was once a substantial two-storey station building and extensive goods yard here. Nearby, the mid-17th century Ewood Hall is one of the area's most attractive buildings, still with stone mullioned and transomed windows.

A final crossing of the Irwell brings the train to Rawtenstall, where only the platform remained for use by the ELR – everything else had to be reconstructed to reflect the 1950s and 1960s ambience that the ELR strives to convey. The town itself has much to attract visitors, including a museum in a former mill-owner's mansion at Whitaker Park, a countryside centre and Britain's last remaining temperance bar.

A major extension of the railway is expected to open in late 2000 – this is the 7.2-km (4½-mile) link between Bury (Bolton Street) and Heywood to the east, which was laid in 1993 but used only for transferring locomotives and rolling stock between the ELR and Railtrack. A package of grants amounting to £1.2 million is enabling the ELR to build a two-platform station at Heywood, re-signal Bolton Street station, repair the seven-arch Roch Viaduct and extend platforms at Rawtenstall to accommodate nine-coach trains.

Fortunately the ELR has a large fleet of locomotives capable of pulling such trains. Most are LMS engines that could have been seen working over the ELR under British Railways, but there are a few 'strangers' such as the unique Riddles Pacific *Duke of Gloucester*, the A4 named after its designer, *Sir Nigel Gresley*, and a Great Western Railway 2-8-2 tank that spent most of its life at Severn Tunnel Junction and Newport in South Wales.

EMBSAY STEAM RAILWAY

Serving the Craven district of the Yorkshire Dales, the picturesque Midland Railway (MR) line from Skipton to Ilkley was a relative latecomer, being opened in 1887–8. Apart from linking small Dales communities with the larger towns at each end, it also carried some longer-distance trains such as the Manchester–Ilkley trains operated by the Lancashire & Yorkshire Railway and MR trains from Colne to Harrogate. It even served as a diversionary route for such trains as the 'Thames–Clyde Express' when work on the Aire Valley line compelled the re-routing of trains between Leeds and the Settle & Carlisle line.

Despite early dieselization of the line in 1959, the economics of the line did not survive Dr Beeching's scrutiny and the route was closed in 1965, except for the short section between Skipton and the divergence

of the branch to Grassington, which still serves an important Tilcon quarry at Rylstone. Before the future of this quarry became assured, the equally scenic Grassington branch was the object of the Embsay and Grassington Preservation Society, and their move to Embsay was originally intended as a temporary base.

▶The Embsay & Bolton Abbey Steam Railway relies on its large number of industrial locomotives, like Barclay 0-4-0 saddle tank No 22 of 1952, rather than ex-BR engines.

When the decision was taken to develop Rylstone, the society changed its name to the Yorkshire Dales Railway (YDR) and turned its attention to the line on from Embsay to Bolton Abbey. The remains of this Augustinian foundation have attracted visitors for centuries, and the nave was being restored for services by Augustus Pugin when the railway was in its infancy.

The first trains ran over a short section of track at Embsay in 1979, and it was not until 1997 that the final extension to Bolton Abbey was opened, turning the YDR into a useful transport link as well as a showcase for the railway's large collection of industrial

EMBSAY STEAM RAILWAY

Length of line: *7.2km (4½ miles)*
Operating periods:
  Every Sunday; Saturdays in June and September;
  daily late July–end August.
Facilities: *Buffet, tea room, shop.*
Access for disabled:
  Access to Embsay and Bolton Abbey; special toilets
  at Bolton Abbey.
Public transport: *Pennine bus from Skipton.*
Nearby tourist attractions:
  Skipton Castle, Bolton Abbey, Barden Tower,
  Upper Dales Folk Museum.
Address:
  Bolton Abbey Station, Bolton Abbey, Skipton,
  North Yorkshire BD23 6AF.
Telephone (information): *01756 794727*
Telephone (timetable): *01756 795189*

steam locomotives. The award that was given for the reconstruction of Bolton Abbey station reflects the care with which the extension has been carried out.

In contrast, the YDR inherited the original station buildings and tall signal box at Embsay, the former now housing an outstanding collection of books for sale about railways and industrial archaeology. Trains head east out of Embsay through the broad, open valley, the fields delineated by dry stone walls. From Holywell Halt (request stop), there is a children's trail and a picnic area. Passing under a main road the train enters a rocky cutting to reach the loop at Stoneacre, which was the temporary terminus of the line until 1997. There is no passenger access here.

There is much to do from the station at Bolton Abbey, apart from visiting the abbey itself. A wetland area near the station is being developed to foster the

➥Trains from Bolton Abbey run through Embsay to Bow Bridge loop, where Hunslet J94 0-6-0 saddle tank No 69 is seen running round its train.

growth of indigenous rare plants and flowers such as the bee orchid. The Bolton Abbey Estate is threaded by 120km (75 miles) of footpaths, including access to the chasm of the River Wharfe known as 'the Strid'.

Trains return through Embsay to Bow Bridge loop close to the junction of the Grassington branch, which can be seen as the engine runs round for the return to Embsay.

GROUDLE GLEN RAILWAY

This delightful 610-mm (2-ft) gauge railway was built as part of the late-Victorian development of the Isle of Man's tourist attractions. It was built to take visitors from a station named Lhen Coan near the Groudle Hotel through a narrow valley on to the headland and along the coast to Sea Lion Rocks station. Here sea lions

*The 2-4-0 tank **Polar Bear** was built by WG Bagnall Ltd in 1905. When the railway closed, it was bought for £25 and now works at the Amberley Chalk Pits Museum in Sussex.*

GROUDLE GLEN RAILWAY

Length of line: *1.2km (¾ mile)*
Operating periods:
Easter Sunday and Monday;
Sundays and Bank Holidays
May–September.
Facilities: *Shop.*
Access for disabled:
Awkward access – please telephone in advance.
Public transport:
Manx Electric Railway.
Location:
Groudle Glen, near Groudle Hotel
(stop of Manx Electric Railway).
Telephone (information):
01624 622138 (evenings);
01624 670453 (weekends)

Sea Lion Rocks station on the Groudle Glen Railway, overlooking the Irish Sea. The sea lion pool and polar bear enclosure were once located in the inlet below the station.

were put through the indignities of performing tricks for visitors. The glen was even lit by coloured fairy lights when electric lighting was still uncommon, and a network of paths linked by rustic bridges led to other attractions such as swings and a dance floor.

The line opened in 1896 and was so successful that extra carriages and another steam locomotive had to be ordered to cope with the demand for up to 40 return trips a day. Having survived two world wars, the line finally closed in 1963 when the last working steam locomotive was worn out. The two Bagnall 2-4-0 tank locomotives, *Polar Bear* and *Sea Lion*, were sold, the track taken up and sold for scrap and the buildings demolished. *Polar Bear* found its way to the Amberley Chalk Pits Museum in West Sussex, where it

can be seen at work, although it made a special return to its original haunt in 1993.

The plan to restore the Groudle Glen Railway (GGR) was formally launched in 1982, and four years later the section as far as the headland was reopened with a diesel locomotive. The remains of *Sea Lion* were found in Loughborough and the locomotive was restored by instructors and apprentices at the BNFL Training Centre at Sellafield in Cumbria. The engine returned to the GGR in 1987. Five years later the spectacular stretch overlooking the Irish Sea was brought back into use, and the Swiss-chalet style station building at Lhen Coan has been rebuilt, just as it was when the glen received over 100,000 visitors a year.

Before the delightful signals were removed from the station at Douglas, 2-4-0 tank No 4 Loch waits to leave for Peel. No 4 was the last engine to be overhauled before closure in 1968.

Horse-drawn trams began trotting between Douglas's Victoria Pier and Derby Castle in 1892. The 3.2km (2 miles) is level, and about 50 horses haul three different types of car.

ISLE OF MAN STEAM RAILWAY

The Isle of Man was once served by an extensive 914mm (3ft) gauge network, built largely on the prospect of profits from the tourist industry. Between 1873 and 1879 main lines were opened from the capital at Douglas to Peel, Port Erin and Ramsey, followed by a short branch to Foxdale, where the most productive lead and silver workings in the British Isles were then to be found. After a difficult start financially, the railways flourished, with a huge influx of visitors as the 19th century neared its close. The number of passengers continued to increase after the First World War to reach a total of 1,609,155 in 1920.

Small wonder that a fleet of 16 locomotives was required to operate the train services, which reached 100 departures a day from Douglas at the height of the railway's prosperity. However, bus, coach and motor cars began to erode traffic, and the Depression reduced the numbers of visitors still further. A gradual decline set in, although matters improved briefly during the 1950s. Despite the valiant efforts of the Marquess of Ailsa to save the entire Isle of Man Railway (IOMR) system, the last public trains ran to Ramsey and Peel in 1968. The survival of even the Port Erin line looked doubtful for some years, until wiser councils in the island's Parliament, the Tynwald, won the case for the line's purchase by the government.

Although Douglas station has lost much of its appeal with the removal of one of its two island platforms and the destruction of the elegant canopies that stretched the length of the platforms, the journey

ISLE OF MAN STEAM RAILWAY

Length of line: *24.8km (15½ miles)*
Operating periods:
 Daily Easter–September; last week of October.
Facilities: *Buffet, shops, museum.*
Access for disabled:
 Special carriages for wheelchairs; ramps; level access at Douglas and Port Erin.
Public transport: *Buses to main centres.*
Nearby tourist attractions:
 Castletown Nautical Museum, Castle Rushen, Marine Biological Station (Port Erin), Manx Museum (Douglas).
Address:
 Isle of Man Railways, Strathallan Crescent, Douglas, Isle of Man IM2 4NR.
Telephone (information): *01624 663366*

that has delighted generations of holidaymakers remains unspoilt. After a climb through Nunnery Woods, the line reaches the cliffs at Keristal above Port Soderick, with wonderful views over the Irish Sea. The station building at Port Soderick, built like all the stations on the Port Erin line of distinctive rich red Ruabon brick, seems bewilderingly massive, but the coast here was so popular with holidaymakers that special short workings had to be run from Douglas.

The line turns inland for the climb up to Santon, the highest point on the line, before dropping down through farm and woodland to Ballasalla and the island's former capital at Castletown. It was here that a winter evening passenger train went through the goods shed doors when someone forgot to reset the points for the main line. The station is well situated for exploration of this historic town.

➼ *One of the former County Donegal Railway railcars, bought in the early 1960s, leaves Douglas station. Its character was later ruined by the destruction of its platform canopies.*

Double-headed trains were common on the Isle of Man, running boat and mail trains, sometimes non-stop. Here No 1 **Sutherland** *and No 6* **Peveril** *wait to leave Douglas in 1955.*

The line continues through the tiny station at Colby and the much larger affair at Port St Mary to the terminus at Port Erin, where there is a railway museum with a varying selection of the IOMR's engines. It used to include the oldest – No 1 Sutherland of 1873, named after the 3rd Duke of *Sutherland* who was keenly interested in railways and the IOMR's first chairman – but it was returned to service in 1998.

The railway is still operated by the locomotives built for it by Beyer Peacock and Dübs. Only one of the 16 original locomotives has been scrapped though one, No 3 *Pender*, has been sectioned for the North West Museum of Science & Industry in Manchester to show how a steam engine works. One other locomotive is in private hands, but 13 are still on the railway after a history spanning over 120 years.

KEIGHLEY & WORTH VALLEY RAILWAY

The television and film industries have come to rely heavily on heritage railways for 'instant' sets, just as they rely on the National Trust and English Heritage for country house or castle settings. In all cases this provides welcome funds to further worthy causes. Of all the films and programmes that have been made on heritage railways, probably the best-known is *The Railway Children*, made in 1970 and based on E Nesbitt's 1906 classic story. Its fame was a tremendous help to the fledgling railway around which it was filmed, the Keighley & Worth Valley Railway (KWVR) in West Yorkshire.

The KWVR was one of the early preserved railways, opening in 1968, six years after British Railways closed the former Midland Railway (MR) branch. It was built to link the mills, factories and villages of the Worth Valley with the Leeds–Carlisle main line at Keighley, and was constructed with

The hills around Haworth provided the Brontë sisters with the settings for some of their novels. GWR pannier tank No 5775 leaves Haworth on a Christmas holiday working.

earthworks wide enough for a second track to be laid, such was the optimism about its prospects. The railway opened in 1867 – too late for any of the Brontë family who lived at the parsonage in Haworth – but their fame and the museum devoted to them that was opened in 1895 helped to generate additional traffic on the branch, which had a service of 17 daily passenger trains each way at its height.

The frequent and fast train services to Keighley from Leeds, Bradford and Skipton make it easy to reach the KWVR without sitting in a traffic jam. Keighley station still has the atmosphere of an important junction station with its large covered overbridge and wide ramps. The KWVR platforms are covered by a long glazed canopy, which shelters various shops and a period bookstall, as well as a profusion of hanging baskets. At the south end is a turntable rescued from Garsdale on the Settle &

KEIGHLEY & WORTH VALLEY RAILWAY

Length of line: *7.6km (4¾ miles)*
Operating periods:
Every weekend and Bank Holiday;
daily mid-June–early September.
Facilities: *Buffet, real ale bar on most steam trains, shops, museums.*
Access for disabled: *Wheelchairs accommodated in guard's compartment with advance notice.*
Public transport: *Keighley station.*
Nearby tourist attractions:
Cliffe Castle Museum, East Riddlesden Hall (NT), Haworth Parsonage, Haworth Museum of Childhood.
Address:
Haworth Station, Keighley,
West Yorkshire BD22 8NJ.
Telephone (information): *01535 645214*
Telephone (timetable): *01535 647777*

Carlisle line in 1989 to fill the pit left empty by the removal of its identical predecessor. The beautifully constructed stone-based water tower still supplies the column at the end of the platform, and the signal box from Esholt Junction near Shipley stands on the same site as an earlier vandalized box.

The line climbs all the way from Keighley to Oakworth, and begins with a 1 in 58 gradient that defeated the inaugural train in 1867. The railway crosses over the former Great Northern Railway (GNR) goods branch, followed by the now tree-covered site of GN Junction where a spur went off to join the line to Ingrow East and Queensbury. Ingrow West is the first station on the KWVR and has undergone as great a transformation as any on a heritage railway. For many years after the railway reopened it was near-derelict, with no buildings, but in the mid-1980s it was rejuvenated by the re-erection of the attractive stone station building from Foulbridge on the Colne–Skipton line. Oil lamps were installed, the environs were tidied up and the station drive was graced with a pair of gates from Keighley Midland goods yard.

In the goods yard a museum building was put up to house the outstanding collection of coaches built up by the Vintage Carriages Trust: these include the magnificent Great Central Railway four-wheeled composite coach of 1876 and the GNR six-wheeler of 1888. Some of the older vehicles had been relegated by BR to use by permanent waygangs and lacked any of their finer fittings, making the standard of their restoration an even greater accomplishment.

Once through Ingrow Tunnel, the line passes some tall mill buildings before arriving at the tiny station of Damens, reputed to have been the smallest in the country. An equally modest signal box from Earby Crossing on the Colne–Skipton line has been added to the hen-coop-sized station. People on a nearby housing estate that has no bus service use the halt for transport, reflecting the way the KWVR has benefited several of the local communities by providing public transport. Beyond the station is a passing loop put in by volunteers in 1970 to increase the line's capacity. The MR signal box was moved as a single unit from

◀ *BR Class 4MT 2-6-4 tank No 80002 waits to leave Haworth station in a carefully re-created picture of the early 1950s British Railways, with the 'cycling lion' emblem.*

Frizinghall on the Shipley–Bradford line, and most of the signals are authentic MR examples.

Oakworth station was the domain of Mr Perks in *The Railway Children*. It was one of the first stations on any heritage railway to be so meticulously restored, and set the standard for others to follow. Gas lamps (the station has never had electricity) and coal fires in the grates help to create an evocative atmosphere as night falls, especially when a train adds clouds of steam on a cold day.

After Oakworth the line used to cross over a millpond by an elaborate trestle structure, but in 1892 the MR built a new route that required construction of the three-arch Mytholmes Viaduct and 69-m (75-yd) Mytholmes Tunnel. Its portal has been a favourite vantage point for photographers and is reached by a footpath that crosses the tunnel.

☛Oxenhope in winter, when the absence of people and short trains make for a very different atmosphere from the bustle of summer weekends.

The large two-storey goods shed and small station building at Haworth says much about the economics of the Victorian railway. The goods shed has formed the core of the KWVR's engine shed and workshops, though engines awaiting engineering work or restoration can also be found at Oxenhope. Many still arrive at Haworth for the Brontë connections, as they have since 1895, and the station is the busiest on the line. On summer Sundays a bus links the station with the parsonage.

The final stretch between Haworth and Oxenhope is the prettiest on the line, as it follows the Bridgehouse Beck, crossed by a 19th-century packhorse bridge. This lovely stone arch is on the Railway Children Walk, devised by the KWVR to take in some of the places used in making the film. The walk also includes Bents House (The Three Chimneys of the film), which is visible from the line.

The terminus at Oxenhope, which like all the other stations has a single platform, was transformed

by having the approach road relaid with stone setts. This was an early measure of help by Bradford Metropolitan Borough Council to improve the appearance of tourist sites. One of the two sheds behind the station holds stored locomotives; the other is used for carriage restorations and maintenance.

The majority of the KWVR's locomotives are of London Midland & Scottish Railway ancestry, which might have been seen on the branch or at least passing through Keighley on the main line. But there are a few strangers, such as the USA Army Transportation Corps 2-8-0 from Poland, which proved useful in the filming of *Yanks*; a Great Western pannier tank; and an 0-6-2 tank from the Taff Vale Railway, which spent its life hauling coal trains in South Wales.

KIRKLEES LIGHT RAILWAY

Not many railways can claim to have built all their engines in their own workshops, but the Kirklees Light Railway (KLR) is one of them. It obviously helps that the KLR is built to only 381mm (15in) gauge, but that hardly diminishes the achievement, especially when one of them is an articulated 0-4-4-0.

The route of the KLR is the trackbed of a former Lancashire & Yorkshire Railway branch that ran from Clayton West Junction on the Huddersfield–Sheffield line to Clayton West. Construction was hampered by problems with the 465-m (511-yd) Shelley Woodhouse Tunnel, but the line finally opened in 1879. Coal was always the principal traffic (sidings from Clayton West and the only intermediate station at Skelmanthorpe served two collieries), and it was surprising that passenger services lasted until 1983, when the line shut entirely.

➥ *Based on locomotive supplied by Hunslet to India, the* **Kirklees Light Railway's 2-6-2 tank Fox** *was built to half scale with Walschaerts valve gear and completed in 1990.*

KIRKLEES LIGHT RAILWAY

KIRKLEES LIGHT RAILWAY

Length of line: *6.4km (4 miles)*
Operating periods: *Every weekend; daily Spring Bank Holiday–early September.*
Facilities: *Buffet, shop.*
Access for disabled: *Limited.*
Public transport:
Huddersfield station and bus 235; Wakefield station and bus 484; or Denby Dale station.
Nearby tourist attractions:
Yorkshire Sculpture Park.
Address:
Park Mill Way, Clayton West, Nr Huddersfield, West Yorkshire HD8 9XJ.
Telephone (information): *01484 865727*

◆*Brighton-built Fairburn 2-6-4 tank No 42085 spent most of its career in the north east, including two spells at Whitby shed. It was withdrawn in 1967 and bought for preservation.*

With the support of Kirklees Metropolitan Council, Brian Taylor and a growing band of volunteers have established a thriving railway, which has been progressively reopened between 1991 and 1998. The line offers fine views of the South Pennine foothills and Emley Moor Television Mast, the contrast of ancient Blacker Wood, the excitement of Shelley Woodhouse Tunnel and the miniature lines of the Barnsley Society of Model Engineers. The line terminates close to the site of Clayton West Junction, and there has even been a suggestion that there might be an interchange station one day, which would be a first for a 381-mm (15-in) gauge railway.

LAKESIDE & HAVERTHWAITE RAILWAY

Lake Windermere has strong associations with the children's novels written by Arthur Ransome. Some of the scenes that inspired Ransome, and the hotel where he wrote his best-known work *Swallows and Amazons*, pass by the windows of trains on the Lakeside & Haverthwaite Railway (LHR).

The popularity of the Lake District was fostered by the Lake poets Wordsworth, Coleridge and Southey. However, Wordsworth was none too keen on the Kendal & Windermere Railway, the first line that ran to the area's largest lake. The LHR is based on the second line to the lake shore, built by the Furness Railway (FR) from Plumpton Junction to Lakeside and opened in 1869. The railway carried heavy summer traffic from the junction station at Ulverston,

but was quiet for most of the year (unless the lake froze, when hoards of skaters came). There was a surprising amount of freight, principally from a factory producing ultramarine (Reckitt's Blue) and the Backbarrow Iron Works near Haverthwaite, and it was this that kept the line open for two more years after passenger services were withdrawn in 1965.

It took until 1973 to reopen the branch north of Haverthwaite after the short-sighted severance of the southern part by a road scheme. The LHR's main station is Haverthwaite, peculiarly sited between two unlined tunnels with the point into the loop starting before the exit from the southern tunnel. Here the LHR's fleet of

➤Haverthwaite station on the Lakeside & Haverthwaite Railway is most unusually sited between two tunnels. BR-built Fairburn 2-6-4 tank No 42085 enters the flower-fringed station.

LAKESIDE & HAVERTHWAITE RAILWAY

Length of line: *5.6km (3½ miles)*
Operating periods:
  Easter; daily early May–end October.
Facilities: *Buffet, shop.*
Access for disabled: *Limited.*
Public transport: *Lakeside steamers.*
Nearby tourist attractions:
  Stott Park Bobbin Mill, Fell Foot Park.
Address:
  Haverthwaite Station, Near Ulverston,
  Cumbria LA12 8AL.
Telephone (information): *015395 31594*

tank locomotives and stock are kept and maintained.

The journey to Lakeside is as delightful as one would expect of the region, with marvellous views of the surrounding hills, the Leven valley with its waterfall and adjacent mill, the headwaters of the River Leven as it leaves the lake, and Lake Windermere itself. The Newby Bridge Hotel where Ransome stayed and wrote is a short walk from the only station on the line, Newby Bridge Halt. Sadly the magnificent station built by the FR for its patrons to dine to the sounds of an orchestra with harp and bass viol was torn down before the LHR could save it.

➤Laxey on the Manx Electric Railway in 1955, with vestibuled saloon No 7, built in 1894 with a body by Mylnes, and cross-bench open trailer No 48, built in 1899, again with Mylnes body.

◆ *MER winter saloon No 20, built in 1899. The MER opened in 1902. In the same year, Edward VII and Queen Alexandra boarded it to travel from Ramsey to Douglas and back.*

An impression of the elegance of that age on the lake can be obtained, however, from the boat that Ransome immortalized as the houseboat in *Swallows and Amazons* – the *Esperance*. It is now in the Windermere Steam Boat Museum, but once carried its owner, H W Schneider, from his home at Bowness to Lakeside to take the train into his office in Barrow, enjoying breakfast as he steamed down the lake.

MANX ELECTRIC RAILWAY

So much remains of a rich railway heritage that 1993 was designated the 'Year of Railways' on the Isle of Man to commemorate the centenary of the opening of the Manx Electric Railway (MER). Although the 914mm (3ft) gauge MER was the focus of the celebrations, all the island's railways took part and attracted tens of thousands of additional visitors to the island during the summer months.

The first section of the MER as far as Groudle first opened in 1893, beginning at Derby Castle to the

Glen Railway (see page 197). In 1894 the MER was extended to Laxey, famous for its enormous waterwheel of 22m (72ft) diameter built to pump water out of the lead mines under Snaefell. Ramsey was eventually reached by the MER in 1899, and there is now a museum devoted to the MER near the station. Built along the east coast of the island, the MER provides a continually changing panorama over the Irish Sea for 27km (17 miles) and also provides access to the Snaefell Mountain Railway (see page 225).

▲ The interior of MER winter saloon No 19, built by GF Milnes of Birkenhead. The MER is probably unique in being a late 19th-century system still operated by its original stock.

north-east of Douglas. Derby Castle is the terminus of Britain's only surviving horse-drawn tramway, which begins at Douglas's Victoria Pier, and Groudle was a popular destination for the hotel and the Groudle

MANX ELECTRIC RAILWAY

Length of line: *28km (17½ miles)*
Operating periods: *Daily Easter–October;*
   limited service November–March.
Facilities: *Buffet, shop.*
Access for disabled: *Advance notice required.*
Public transport: *Buses to main centres.*
Nearby tourist attractions:
   Groudle Glen Railway, Manx Electric Railway.
Address:
   Isle of Man Railways, Strathallan Crescent,
   Douglas, Isle of Man IM2 4NR.
Telephone (information): *01624 663637*

MIDDLETON RAILWAY

The environs of the Middleton Railway (MR), off an undistinguished side street within earshot of the M1, do nothing to suggest that it once had a formative influence during the Industrial Revolution and is therefore an important heritage site. The MR was the first railway to be authorized by Act of Parliament and the first anywhere in the world to use steam power commercially, in 1812.

The purpose of the 1245mm (4ft 1in) gauge MR was to take coal from the mines at Middleton to barges on the River Aire. Opened in 1758, it was simply a horse-drawn tramway until the agent of the Middleton Estates, John Blenkinsop, came up with the idea of a steam locomotive that would propel itself

In North Eastern Railway green livery, Y7 0-4-0 tank No 1310 passes Y1/2 Sentinel No 68153 on the Middleton Railway. Nineteen Y7s were built in 1888–97 and five more in 1923.

along by a huge toothed wheel that engaged a rack on one of the rails (at that time there was no confidence in the adhesive weight of a locomotive being adequate for propulsion).

All that remains of this extraordinary railway is a set of wheels in the National Railway Museum at York – although an engine was set aside for preservation, it was cut up in 1860. In 1881 the MR was converted to standard gauge and new lines were built to serve nearby factories, creating a network of about 6.4km (4 miles). When in 1958 the new owner of the MR, the National Coal Board, sought to close the parts serving other industries, a group from Leeds University formed what became the Middleton Railway Trust (MRT).

From 1960 the MRT became the first 'preserved' standard gauge line when it took over the goods services, with occasional open days for passengers to ride over the short system – in 1969 they became a regular feature. Demonstration freight trains are also run on certain days to give an idea of the railway's *raison d'être*. The scenery cannot be expected to delight the eye, but landscaping has done much to soften the post-industrial scrubbiness. At the current terminus,

◀ **Mirvale,** *a Hudswell Clarke 0-4-0 saddle tank of 1955, heads along the Balm Road branch of the Middleton Railway. Numerous similar lines once supplied Britain's industries.*

Middleton Park, there is the opportunity to walk in the park once owned by Blenkinsop (his home, Middleton Hall, burned down in 1962) and on into the adjacent woods.

NORTH YORKSHIRE MOORS RAILWAY

The North Yorkshire Moors Railway (NYMR) has an abundance of attributes. It is located in some of the loveliest countryside in Britain, with numerous walks to be enjoyed from its stations and many nearby tourist attractions. Besides being connected to the main railway network, it is long enough at 28.8km (18 miles) to serve a useful transport function, particularly in bringing visitors into the North York Moors National Park. It has a fascinating history, and some of the steepest gradients in railway preservation to tax both the skills of its engine crews and the performance of its fine locomotive fleet.

Situated away from the industrial areas of the north-east that spawned the early tramways and railways, it may seem surprising that the Whitby & Pickering Railway (W&PR) should have been

➥ *Goathland Station on the North Yorkshire Moors has retained its character, and is the starting point for numerous walks, including the famous Roman road on Wheeldale Moor.*

┌─────────────────────────────────┐

MIDDLETON RAILWAY

Length of line: *2km (1¼ miles)*
Operating periods:
   Weekends and Bank Holidays, April–late October.
Facilities: *Shop.*
Access for disabled: *Easy access.*
Public transport:
   Any bus from Corn Exchange to Tunstall Road.
Nearby tourist attractions:
   Abbey House Museum, Armley Mills, Lotherton Hall, Royal Armouries Museum, Temple Newsam House, Thwaite Mills Museum.
Address:
   Moor Road,
   Leeds LS10 2JQ.
Telephone (information): *0113 271 0320*

└─────────────────────────────────┘

amongst the earliest railways in Yorkshire, opening in stages from Whitby to Pickering in 1835–6. The burghers of Whitby were concerned about the contraction in the town's staple industries of shipbuilding, whaling and alum, and thought that a railway would reverse this decline. Accordingly in 1831 they asked the 'father of railways', George Stephenson, to report on the feasibility of a railway constructed for working by animal power.

The line was worked by a combination of horses, stationary steam engines on the section of incline that climbed at gradients of up to 1 in 10 from Beck Hole to Goathland, and gravity. The W&PR remained isolated from the railway system for ten years, until a railway from the south arrived in Pickering in 1845. This prompted the purchase of the W&PR and its conversion to steam traction. This entailed relaying and doubling the track, constructing a larger tunnel at Grosmont (the old one is now a foot tunnel) and replacing bridges. The incline at Beck Hole, however, remained – although the rope was converted from hemp to wire.

Two breaks of the wire in the 1860s (one of which had fatal consequences) prompted the railway's new

---

NORTH YORKSHIRE MOORS RAILWAY

Length of line: *28.8km (18 miles)*
Operating periods: *Daily late March–October.*
Facilities: *Buffets, shops, depot.*
Access for disabled:
Advance notice requested for special attention.
Public transport:
Grosmont station; buses to Pickering from Malton, York and Scarborough.
Nearby tourist attractions:
The Cook Museum (Whitby), Beck Isle Museum of Rural Life (Pickering), Nunnington Hall (NT), Eden Camp (Malton), Wheeldale Roman Road.
Address:
Pickering Station, Pickering, North Yorkshire YO18 7AJ.
Internet address: *http://www.nymr.demon.co.uk*
Telephone (information): *01751 473799*
Telephone (timetable): *01751 472508*

▶ *The NYMR is the only heritage railway to have built a new mechanical cooling plant, seen here with 34072 257 Squadron, visiting from Swanage.*

owner, the North Eastern Railway (NER), to eliminate the incline with a new 8-km (5-mile) section between Grosmont and Goathland, though even this had gradients as steep as 1 in 49. The new section opened in 1865, the same year that the railway was joined at its northern end by the opening of the Esk Valley line to Castleton to link up with the existing line on to Middlesbrough – this is also a delightful journey.

The growth of Whitby as a tourist destination made the line extremely busy during the summer months. A measure of how busy this line once was with excursion traffic to the seaside, as well as local passenger and freight, was the provision of double track between Pickering and Grosmont with no less than 10 signal boxes – High Mill, New Bridge, Farnwarth, Levisham, Newtondale, Summit, Goathland, Deviation, Grosmont Crossing and Grosmont Junction.

Such traffic levels were badly affected by the growth of car ownership, and the Beeching Plan proposed the closure of all railways to Whitby. A successful outcome rarely followed the chorus of protests against railway closures, but the Esk Valley line was saved. The Whitby–Pickering–Rillington line, however, closed in 1965, and moves by several councils to save the line came to nought.

Two years later, with a series of public meetings that attracted strong local support, the NYMR Company was formed. Almost from the beginning, North Yorkshire County Council realized the importance of the line for public transport within the National Park – a role that has become increasingly important as more and more cars clog the lanes and spoil the very tranquillity people come to enjoy. The Council purchased the line and leased it back to the NYMR, enabling the line to be reopened to passengers in stages between 1973 and 1976.

The NYMR's success in attracting visitors to the railway – helped by the popular television series *Heartbeat*, which was shot around Goathland – means that it is often short of capacity on gala days, and is considering reinstating double track for 4.8km (3 miles) on either side of Goathland summit.

The view from Skelton Tower overlooking Newtondale between the eponymous halt and Levisham. The train is headed by BR Class 4MT 2-6-4 tank No 80135, once a Cambrian engine.

Standing on the platform at the junction station of Grosmont, part of the village but bordering woodland, it is hard to imagine that from about 1865 to 1891 there was an ironworks opposite the station big enough to keep four shunting locomotives at work. The level-crossing is protected by an imposing signal box opened in 1996, built with bricks from a demolished signal box in Whitby and fitted with a 52-lever frame from Horden near Hartlepool. From this level-crossing a footpath runs parallel with the railway to the 1836 tunnel, which now leads to the engine shed and workshops. A viewing gallery allows visitors to watch the activity here and to see the first

mechanical coaling plant built in Britain since 1950.

Leaving Grosmont, trains almost immediately enter the double-track tunnel, emerging to pass the engine shed on the left and the site of the junction for the original line to the Beck Hole incline; after the incline closed this line continued in use to serve the isolated hamlet of Beck Hole and nearby ironstone mines. The line begins its formidable climb, the stirring exhaust beat from the locomotive continuing all the way to Goathland. As the line climbs, the views to the right broaden before the line burrows into the woods that fringe the line through the long S-curve that precedes the final straight into Goathland.

This wonderfully preserved NER station has all its original buildings, including the elegantly shaped locomotive water columns and the remains of the coal staithes that were such a feature of this company's stations. An unusually straight section of track takes the line into the moors, a landscape punctuated by occasional farm buildings and inhabited by sheep

▲Apart from the panelled rooms, oak and pine staircase and lovely gardens, the late 17th-century house of Nunnington has an incomparable collection of miniature rooms in dolls' houses.

rather than people. The curious tower on the horizon to the east is the replacement for the better-known 'golf balls' of Fylingdales Early Warning Station.

The climb of 152m (500ft) from Grosmont is reached at Fen Bog, after which the line descends towards Pickering. To cross this bog, the railway's builders had to employ the kind of techniques used by the great engineer Joseph Mitchell in the Highlands, using heather bundles, trees and moss-covered hurdles to create a firm foundation. Newtondale Halt is the starting point for some of the most popular walks in the National Park, and leaflets are available as well as the information boards at most stations.

The line descends at grades as steep as 1 in 49 through the narrow valley of Newtondale, the trees emphasizing the feeling of the railway being hemmed

◀*BR Class 4MT 2-6-4 tank No 80135 passes under the elegant three-arched bridge at Darnholm with the 9.15am from Grosmont, banked by Class J72 0-6-0 tank No 69023.*

in by the steep valley sides. Overlooking the line is the Victorian folly of Skelton's Tower, put up in about 1850 by an eponymous clergyman who is supposed to have taken inspiration from the view for his sermons. Fit walkers can enjoy the same prospect by reaching it on a footpath from the next station at Levisham, another delightfully remote spot that has had a starring role in many films. The stationmaster's house is curiously positioned at right angles to the line and one corner intrudes on the platform as though the house was here before the railway and there was no possibility of moving the line a few feet to the east; in fact, it dates from the opening of the original line in 1836.

The line's longest straight takes the train to Farwath, a few cottages that often had to depend on the railway for lifts into Pickering, despite the absence of a formal station or halt. Sharp curves at Kingthorpe precede the approach to Pickering and the permanent way depot at New Bridge that controls the colour light signalling – the only dissonant note on the line. A trout farm and the 14th-century castle can be seen before the train draws into Pickering station, well placed for an exploration of the attractive town. Until 1952 the station was graced with an overall roof, and there are plans to replace it.

It has long been an ambition of the NYMR to operate trains to Whitby and in 1999 an agreement was reached that will give even more scope for the railway's impressive fleet of locomotives, which has several of NER origin and examples from all four pre-nationalization companies. The fleet includes the famous A2 Pacific *Blue Peter*, and a pair of powerful 2-10-0s, which both saw service in Egypt.

RAVENGLASS & ESKDALE RAILWAY

The Ravenglass & Eskdale Railway (RER) has the longest railway history of any miniature line in the country and incontestably offers the finest scenery to be seen from a 381-mm (15-in) gauge carriage. The RER, which is entirely situated within the Lake District National Park, runs from the small seaside village of Ravenglass alongside the River Mite and skirts the eastern flank of Muncaster Fell to enter

◆Ravenglass & Eskdale 2-8-2 River Mite, built in the 1960s by Clarksons of York using parts of the tender from the 1923 River Esk. She is seen here at journey's end at Dalegarth.

Eskdale, terminating at Dalegarth within sight of the Hardknott Pass.

The origins of the railway lie in the haematite that was dug in Eskdale even before the Romans arrived. From the 1870s the voracious appetite for raw materials in the ironworks of Barrow and Workington raised the price of iron ore. To link the revived mines of Eskdale with the Barrow–Carlisle railway line at Ravenglass, a 914mm (3ft) line was built and opened for goods in 1875. The first passengers were carried the following year, but demand for seats from tourists sometimes exceeded the railway's limited capacity, so seats were rigged up in open wagons. Within six months the RER was in receivership. In 1908 a letter to the head of the Board of Trade, Winston Churchill, complaining about the state of the track, deprived the

railway of the right to carry passengers and in 1913 it finally gave up the struggle and closed.

That would probably have been the last of the 'Ratty', as it had become affectionately known, had it not been for the pioneering model maker and architect from Northampton, W J Bassett-Lowke. In 1915 he and his partner Robert Proctor Mitchell were searching for a suitable site to build a more extensive miniature railway than their previous ventures at the seaside or in parks. Even before a lease of the Ratty was signed, they started relaying the line to 381mm (15in) gauge and trains as far as Muncaster Mill started running in August. By the following summer the old terminus at Boot had been reached to serve the iron- ore mines, but the line was cut back to Beckfoot when these closed. The only subsequent alteration to the route was the creation of a new terminus at Dalegarth by using the trackbed of the Gill Force branch as far as the main road up Eskdale; this was more convenient and conspicuous than the old site below Dalegarth Cottages.

RAVENGLASS & ESKDALE RAILWAY

Length of line: *11.2km (7 miles)*
Operating periods:
  Daily late March–late October.
Facilities: *Buffets, shops, museum.*
Access for disabled:
  Special coaches for wheelchairs (advance notice requested); special toilets at Ravenglass and Eskdale.
Public transport: *Ravenglass station.*
Nearby tourist attractions:
  Muncaster Castle, Water Mill.
Address:
  Ravenglass, Cumbria CA18 1SW.
Telephone (information): *01229 717171*

Granite quarries provided substantial stone traffic to augment passenger income, and the line continued to carry stone during the Second World War. Passenger traffic recommenced after VE Day, but the line was put up for sale by the quarry company in 1958. Low levels of maintenance meant that a large outlay was required to bring the Ratty up to standard, and, unfortunately, no one came forward. A mere month's notice of the auction of the line – in 60 lots if necessary – galvanized people into action. The RER Preservation Society was formed, raising £5000, and the balance of the £12,000 final bid was found by a Midlands stockbroker, Colin Cartwright.

The world's oldest working 381-mm (15-in) gauge locomotive in the world: **River Irt, built in 1894 as** Muriel **by Sir Arthur Heywood at his Derbyshire home, is seen at Dalegarth.**

▲ The Ratty in the 1920s, with 2-8-2 River Esk *standing beneath the old station roof at Ravenglass. Designed by Henry Greenly, the engine was built by Davey, Paxman in 1923.*

With Douglas Ferreira as general manager, the Ratty began to be restored to health and developed into one of the Lake District's principal tourist attractions. Stations were enlarged, and the workshops built locomotives for export to Japan as well as for the Ratty. The railway also devised a radio signalling system that British Rail examined when it was looking to install a comparable system of train control in the Highlands during the 1980s.

The most agreeable way of reaching the Ratty is the picturesque railway around the Cumbrian coast from either Carlisle or Barrow/Lancaster. An imaginatively laid-out museum at Ravenglass gives an introduction to the RER's history, and the railway atmosphere of the station has been created by the use of components from Cumbrian stations. The delightful seats with cast-iron supports of squirrels eating grapes was the idea of the Furness Railway, which built most of the railways in southern Cumbria.

Leaving Ravenglass, trains pass the engine shed, one of the few buildings surviving from 914mm (3ft) gauge days, though the height of the overbridges is a constant reminder of the Ratty's antecedents. After curving to the right the railway reaches the request stop at Muncaster Mill. Restored with the help of Science Museum grants, the mill is open for visitors to watch the daily production of stone-ground organic flour, which is for sale along with other organic products.

The climb through Mill Wood is at 1 in 42, and it was not unknown for passengers to get out and push the train if the locomotive 'lost its feet' and slipped to a stand. Waiting passengers at Miteside Halt at the summit of the gradient have an upturned boat in which to shelter. The line continues under the northern flank of Muncaster Fell, passing the clearly visible remains of the stone-crushing plant at Murthwaite, which once provided so much traffic for the railway.

The line climbs again, with a brief descent after Walk Mill Summit up to Irton Road station, with views ahead of England's second highest mountain, Scafell (964m/3162ft). Astonishing as it may seem, during the 1920s Irton Road was served by slip coaches, detached at speed from a non-stop train. In common with all RER stations, Irton Road offers walkers various footpaths across the fells, and these walks are described in a booklet *Walks from Ratty* by the doyen of writers for walkers, Alfred Wainwright.

He regarded Eskdale as 'the finest of all valleys for those whose special joy is to travel on foot'.

The line turns south around the flank of Muncaster Fell before resuming an eastward course along Eskdale to the Green station, serving an Outward Bound school. The line's steepest grade of 1 in 36 follows before the passing loop at Fisherground, where a water supply for the engines is taken from an old mine adit. The largest earthwork on the RER, known as Gilbert's Cutting after Colin Gilbert, was cut in 1964 to avoid a severe reverse curve that did nothing for tyre wear. After Beckfoot there is another steep rise past the point at which the original line proceeded to the mines at Boot; the trackbed is now a footpath. The line swings to the right across Whillan Beck to terminate at Eskdale/Dalegarth station.

The five principal working steam locomotives include the world's oldest working 381mm (15in) gauge locomotive, the 0-8-2 *River Irt*, which began life in 1894 as an 0-8-0 tank on the Duffield Bank Railway in Derbyshire. It was built by Sir Arthur

Heywood as part of his campaign to promote the concept of 'minimum gauge railways' for estate and military use, and he is regarded as the progenitor of miniature railways.

SNAEFELL MOUNTAIN RAILWAY

On a clear day you can see four kingdoms from the 620-m (2034-ft) summit of Snaefell, the highest point on the Isle of Man: the Lake District peaks, the Mull of Galloway, Anglesey and Snowdonia, and the Mountains of Mourne in Ireland. Thankfully a road has never been built up the mountain, but the Victorians did build the electric Snaefell Mountain Railway (SMR) for those without the stamina for the climb. The idea was first discussed formally in January

➦ *The Manx Northern Railway, which built the line from St John's to Ramsey, had four engines. No 4 was a Dübs-built 0-6-0 side tank and is seen here at Bungalow on the way to Snaefell.*

SNAEFELL MOUNTAIN RAILWAY

Length of line: *8km (5 miles)*
Operating periods: *Daily May–September.*
Facilities: *Buffet, shops.*
Access for disabled: *Limited.*
Public transport: *Manx Electric Railway.*
Nearby tourist attractions:
Laxey Wheel, Murray's Motorcycle Museum.
Address:
Isle of Man Railways, Strathallan Crescent, Douglas, Isle of Man IM2 4NR.
Telephone (information): *01624 663366*

1895, and with none of the years of feasibility studies and endless reports that attend such projects today, work started the same month and the railway opened to the public in August of the same year.

Oddly, the SMR is built to a gauge of 1067mm (3ft 6in), a different gauge from the Manx Electric Railway (MER, see page 211): the reason was probably to give more space for the equipment associated with the Fell centre rail system adopted for guiding and braking on the severe gradients of up to 1 in 12. The SMR begins in a glade alongside the MER and climbs a vertical height of 555m (1820ft) in 8km (5 miles). It employs the unusual current of 550V, and remains Britain's only electric mountain railway.

SOUTH TYNEDALE RAILWAY

Alston is the highest market town in England, situated in the South Tyne Valley and often cut off in the winter by severe blizzards. The population of the valley was never enough to excite railway

Two of the 1895 vestibuled saloons of the Snaefell Mountain Railway, Nos 2 and 4, pass near the summit. The steep gradients and the need for the Fell Centre rail can be appreciated.

◆South Tynedale Railway mainstay is a Hunslet 0-4-2 tank named Chaka's Kraal No 6, *which was repatriated from South Africa, where it worked on a sugar plantation in Natal.*

promoters, but the lead and coal mines in the area held out the prospect of sufficient traffic to justify a railway from a junction with the Newcastle–Carlisle line at Haltwhistle. This 20.8-km (13-mile) line opened in 1852 and entailed the construction of nine viaducts, some of them impressive and beautifully situated, such as the one at Lambley, recently taken into the care of the Northern Viaducts Trust.

The line closed to goods traffic in 1965 and the last passenger train ran in 1976, three years after the formation of the South Tynedale Railway Preservation Society (STRPS), set up to preserve the railway, or a section of it, after the proposed closure. The costs involved proved too great, and the project was scaled down to a 610mm (2ft) gauge railway.

With help from the English Tourist Board, the first section from Alston to Gilderdale was opened in 1983. Further stretches were relaid to the current terminus at Kirkhaugh, though work is continuing towards the

---

SOUTH TYNEDALE RAILWAY

Length of line: *3.6km (2¼ miles)*
Operating periods:
  Weekends and Bank Holidays April–October; daily Easter week, Spring Bank Holiday week, July and August; Thursdays June and September.
Facilities: *Tea room, shop.*
Access for disabled: *Limited.*
Public transport:
  Haltwhistle station and Wright Bros bus to Alston, Newcastle–Alston–Keswick. Tel: 01228 606000 for all times.
Nearby tourist attractions:
  Killhope Lead Mining Centre, High Mill (waterwheel).
Address:
  The Railway Station, Alston, Cumbria CA9 3JB.
Telephone (information): *01434 381696*
Telephone (timetable): *01434 382828*

former intermediate station of Slaggyford.

Trains leave from beside the imposing old station building at Alston and traverse the valley of stone-walled fields and scattered farms, interrupted by occasional blocks of uniformly planted conifers that are part of commercial forestry operations. The six

➤ *The oldest engine on the Tanfield Railway is the 1873 veteran* **Wellington,** *an 0-4-0 saddle tank built by Black Hawthorn in nearby Gateshead. Many TR coaches are not much younger.*

steam locomotives are a surprisingly cosmopolitan lot, having worked on industrial lines in Natal, Turkey, Spain and Poland before taking passengers along the South Tyne.

TANFIELD RAILWAY

Given its importance in the history of railways, the Tanfield Railway (TR) deserves to be much better known. Not only is it the oldest working railway in the world, but it offers passengers the

opportunity to see the world's oldest surviving railway bridge, situated in a surprisingly picturesque setting for a coal railway. It also has what is thought to be the oldest working engine shed in the world, dating from 1854. The TR is believed to have been opened in stages between 1712 and 1725 to take coal to Dunston Staithes on the Tyne from Tanfield Moor in the County Durham coalfield.

Horses and waggons made almost entirely of wood were the means of transporting the coal until work began in 1839 to rebuild the TR as an iron railway, with steam winding engines or self-acting (balanced) inclines on the steepest sections. Horses were still used on the level parts. The TR became a branch line of the North Eastern Railway (NER), connected to the Bowes Railway (see page 188), and continued in use until 1962. It was this connection to the Bowes Railway, coupled with the continued maintenance of

➥ *The engine shed and workshops at Marley Hill provide the perfect setting for the industrial railway, and their interiors have been used in films of Catherine Cookson's novels.*

TANFIELD RAILWAY

Length of line: *4.8km (3 miles)*
Operating periods:
 Sunday and Bank Holiday weekends January– November; Thursdays and Saturdays late July–end August.
Facilities: *Buffet, shop.*
Access for disabled:
 Access to Andrews House station; special toilet at Causey Arch.
Public transport:
 Bus X30 on weekdays; buses 706, 708, and 722 to Sunniside on Sundays.
Nearby tourist attractions:
 Bowes Railway, Gibside (NT).
Location:
 Marley Hill Engine Shed, Sunniside, Gateshead.
Telephone (information): *0191 274 2002*

locomotives at the TR's engine shed at Marley Hill until 1970, that attracted a group of local enthusiasts to the idea of using it as a centre. The advantage of Marley Hill was the covered accommodation and workshop facilities for an outstanding collection of industrial tank engines that date back to 1873. The majority were either built in the North East or worked in the region.

In 1971 the preservationists moved into the shed at Marley Hill with the objective of relaying the TR. It has been progressively reopened to the southern terminus at East Tanfield, which was reached in 1992. Part of the pleasure of a ride on the TR is the superb collection of vintage carriages, which are all over 100 years old. Many are four- or six-wheeled third class carriages that were sold off by pre-grouping railway

☛*National Coal Board 0-6-0 saddle tank No 49, built by Robert Stephenson & Hawthorn in 1943 climbs through pleasant countryside towards Andrews House with a charter coal train.*

companies as transport for miners, so they are spartan in their comfort; but there are also a few well-appointed inspection or family saloons.

The journey is surprisingly verdant, for almost all traces of the area's industrial past have been erased. Much of the route is through ancient woodland, bisected by paths that give passengers the opportunity of detraining and exploring the Causey Arch and surrounding exhibits, which include a reconstruction of a wooden coal wagon.

WEST LANCASHIRE LIGHT RAILWAY

The West Lancashire Light Railway (WLLR) shares a similar objective to the Leighton Buzzard Railway in trying to convey something of the atmosphere and history of the narrow gauge industrial light railway. The 610mm (2ft) gauge WLLR is based on the site of an old brick works that extracted clay from adjacent pits, linked by a narrow gauge cable-worked railway.

▲ *A photographers' evening on the West Lancashire Light Railway produced this picture of* **Irish Mail**, *a Hunslet 0-4-0 saddle tank that once worked at Dinorwic slate quarries.*

The idea for setting up the railway came from six schoolboy railway enthusiasts in 1967, when tracklaying began at Alty's Brickworks using redundant railway materials found on the site (the brickworks finally closed three years later). It is remarkable how much has since been achieved, thanks to sheer hard work rather than a fat cheque book. For instance, when the locomotives from the quarries at Dinorwic in North Wales were sold in 1969, the WLLR could afford only the frame of one of them. Two years later they managed to buy a boiler from a sister engine, but it was on one of the highest terraces at the Dinorwic quarry. It took six months of effort to get the boiler down the mountain, using a wagon chassis. An attractive station has been built at Becconsall, together with an extensive locomotive and carriage store and a workshop for restoration.

Although the ride is short, the WLLR is situated on a site well covered with trees that mask the remains of its former use. The collection of locomotives includes some gems, including an engine built by Kerr Stuart in Stoke-on-Trent for service in France during the First World War; it was one of the 'Joffre' class and was rescued from a quarry in the Pas de Calais. Besides the rebuilt Welsh quarry engine, now named *Irish Mail*, and another Dinorwic engine, there are two German Orenstein & Koppel 0-4-0 tanks that worked at a coal mine in Utrillas in Spain.

WEST LANCASHIRE LIGHT RAILWAY

Length of line: *0.4km (¼ mile)*
Operating periods:
  Easter weekend and every Sunday to October.
Facilities: *Buffet, shop.*
Access for disabled: *Limited.*
Public transport:
  Preston or Southport station, and then buses 100 and 102 between them.
Location:
  Alty's Brickworks, Station Road, Hesketh Bank, near Preston, Lancashire.
Telephone (information):
  01772 815881/01645 622654

CHAPTER 6
SCOTLAND

*Scotland boasts many of Britain's most scenic railway lines, one of which --
Fort William to Mallaig – is served by daily, stream-hauled trains during the
summer months. Its preserved railways, though few in number, range from the
rugged beauty of the Strathspey Railway to the artery of overseas trade that
brought the Bo'ness & Kinneil Railway into being.*

◀ *The Caledonian Railway 0-6-0, No 828 stands at Boast of
station on the Strathspey Railway. The white boards in front
of the chimney were CR destination indicators.*

▲ *North Eastern Railway J72 0-6-0 side tank leaves Bo'ness
with the signal box from Garnqueen South Junction on the
left and the overall roof from Haymarket in the distance.*

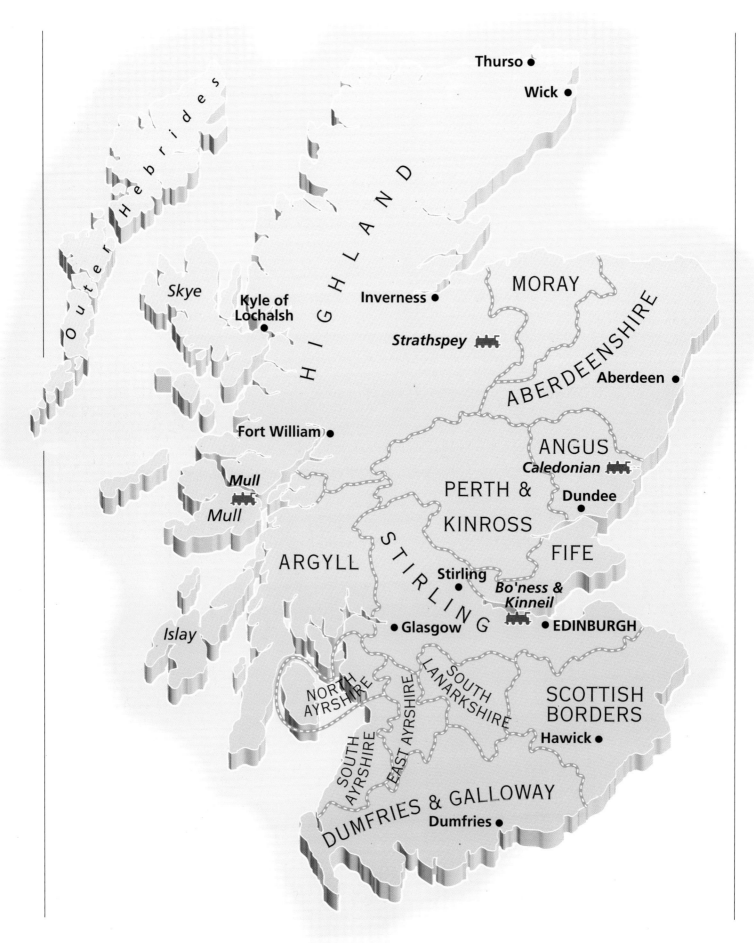

Thurso •

Wick •

Outer Hebrides

H I G H L A N D

Skye

Kyle of
Lochalsh •

Inverness •

MORAY

Strathspey 🚂

ABERDEENSHIRE

Aberdeen •

Fort William •

ANGUS

Caledonian 🚂

PERTH &

Mull 🚂

KINROSS

Dundee •

Mull

FIFE

ARGYLL

S
T
I
R
L
I
N
G

Stirling
•

Bo'ness &
Kinneil

Islay

🚂

Glasgow •

• EDINBURGH

NORTH
AYRSHIRE

SOUTH
LANARKSHIRE

SCOTTISH
BORDERS

EAST AYRSHIRE

Hawick •

SOUTH
AYRSHIRE

DUMFRIES & GALLOWAY

Dumfries •

BO'NESS & KINNEIL RAILWAY

Every heritage railway is testimony to what can be achieved by like-minded individuals pooling their energy, but it would be hard to match the effort and scale of reconstruction at Bo'ness. When members of the Scottish Railway Preservation Society (SRPS) began work here in 1979, there was absolutely nothing but flat ground. Every brick, sleeper, rail and load of ballast, not to mention the buildings, had to be acquired and brought to what has become the fine terminus of the Bo'ness & Kinneil Railway (BKR).

The land was blighted by mining, precluding its use for housing or industry, so the local authority welcomed the idea of a tourist-related project. The SRPS was looking for somewhere to display and use the fine collection of Scottish locomotives and carriages built up

at Falkirk. The idea of the BKR was born, using what little was left of the North British Railway (NBR) branch line that had served the port of Bo'ness from a junction with the Edinburgh–Glasgow main line at Manuel.

The most impressive structure that the SRPS has saved and re-erected at Bo'ness is undoubtedly the important Edinburgh & Glasgow trainshed roof from Haymarket station, dating from 1842. This could not have been achieved without the help of British Rail and Sir Robert McAlpine & Sons. Dating from 1842, the roof is made up of cast- and wrought-iron trusses resting on cast-iron columns. Curiously the roof is of

➤Leaving Bo'ness, the railway sweeps along the foreshore before climbing inland. NBR J36 0-6-0 No 65243 **Maude** *in BR livery works a charter goods train beside the Firth of Forth.*

*◆Giving locomotives a different identity for photographers' specials is a common practice. J36 No 65243 with the alias of No 65233 **Plumer** nears Birkhill station.*

BO'NESS & KINNEIL RAILWAY

Length of line: *5.6km (3½ miles)*
Operating periods:
Weekends early April–mid October; Bank Holidays; daily early July–late August.
Facilities: *Buffets, shop, depot.*
Access for disabled:
Easy access to platform at Bo'ness; special carriage for wheelchairs; special toilets at Bo'ness.
Public transport:
Buses from Linlithgow (nearest station), Falkirk, Stirling, Edinburgh and Glasgow.
Nearby tourist attractions: *Birkhill Clay Mine.*
Address:
Bo'ness Station, Union Street, Bo'ness, West Lothian EH51 9AQ.
Telephone (information): *01506 822298*

timber and Welsh slate, with no vents for smoke.

The station buildings came from Wormit at one end of the Forth Bridge, the footbridge from Murthly at the foot of the Highland main line to Inverness, and the fine Caledonian signal box from Garnqueen South Junction near Coatbridge. The Bo'ness Visitor Trail takes in the attractions of the site and the historical remains of the harbour basin, appropriately lined with ancient wagons, for this was once Scotland's second busiest harbour, principally dealing with coal, iron ore and timber.

The large storage buildings house the SRPS collection built up at Falkirk, which includes examples from all five of Scotland's principal pre-grouping railway companies. Amongst the highlights are a Great North of Scotland Railway bogie saloon that was part of Edward VII's Royal train, the Caledonian Railway 0-4-4 tank and the NBR 0-6-0 named *Maude* after the First World War general.

The journey to Birkhill soon becomes pleasantly rural, once the sight of the vast oil and chemical works at Grangemouth is left behind. The line passes close to the grounds of Kinneil House, where James Watt carried out some of his formative work on the steam engine.

The station at Birkhill is again an entirely new creation, for there was never a station on this site. Passengers are able to visit the fascinating underground workings of the nearby Birkhill Clay Mine, which until 1980 produced clay, some of which was used to produce the brick arches of steam locomotive fireboxes. The tunnels stretch for 9.6km (6 miles) and parties are taken round by retired miners who have a fund of stories to tell. Visitors can see the fossilized remains of trees that were alive 170 million years before the first dinosaurs.

CALEDONIAN RAILWAY

In the town of Brechin, which was settled over 1000 years ago, the terminus of what became a Caledonian Railway (CR) branch from Montrose and Bridge of Dun was opened as early as 1848. Almost 50 years later a line from the west at Forfar was built, opening in 1895 to create a triangular junction at the throat of Brechin station – a most unusual arrangement.

➥ *The use of goods wagons for photographers' charters has given a commercial as well as cosmetic reason for their restoration, as seen in this fine private owners wagon at Bo'ness goods shed.*

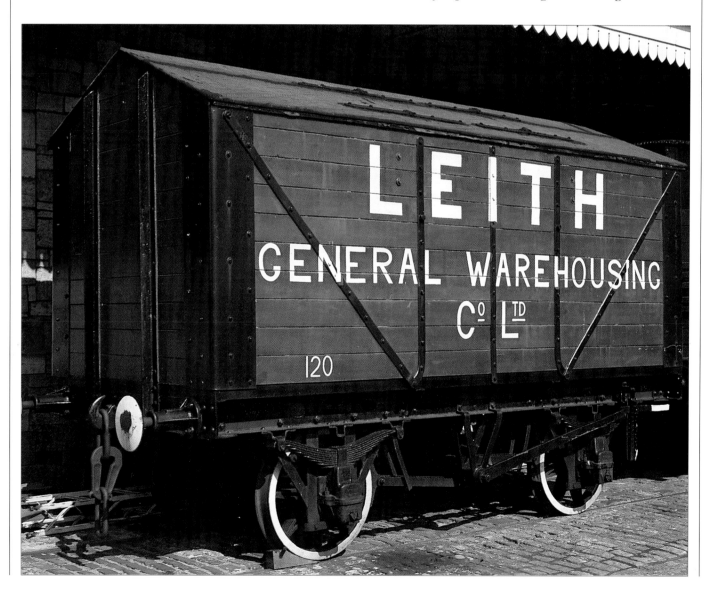

CALEDONIAN RAILWAY

Length of line: *6.4km (4 miles)*
Operating periods:
Easter Sunday; last Sunday in May to first in September.
Facilities: *Buffet, shop, museum, depot.*
Access for disabled:
Ramps at stations; special toilet at Brechin; help with wheelchairs.
Public transport:
Nearest station Montrose; Strathtay Scottish buses from Montrose (01674 672805).
Nearby tourist attractions:
Brechin Castle Centre, Brechin Cathedral, House of Dun (NTS), Montrose Basin Wildlife Centre.
Address:
The Station, 2 Park Road, Brechin, Angus DD9 7AF.
Telephone (information): *01674 810318*
Telephone (timetable): *01356 622992*

The avoiding line at Brechin survived only until 1917, when it was lifted to provide rails for the war effort. Passenger services on both lines must have been poorly patronized for they were withdrawn as early as 1952. Freight services from Kinnaber Junction survived until 1981, releasing the line for the Brechin Preservation Society (BRS), which had been formed two years previously.

The BRS is fortunate in having a very fine Grade B-listed station building, built in 1847–8 for the Aberdeen Railway and extended for the CR in 1894–5 by Thomas Barr when the Forfar line was added. Wood and cast-iron awnings run the length of the single-storey offices on both street and platform sides, and both sides have a clock in a miniature gable surmounted by a ball finial. The station has a small museum. The CR runs from Brechin to the former junction at Bridge of Dun, and has a small collection of industrial locomotives and a British Railways-built Ivatt 2-6-0.

☛ *The J94 Austerity 0-6-0 tank has been a mainstay of the smaller heritage railways. Here Bagnall-built No 6 of 1944 leaves the splendid terminus at Brechin for Bridge of Dun.*

MULL RAILWAY

The principal tourist attraction on the Isle of Mull is Torosay Castle, 3.2km (2 miles) from the pier where the ferries from Oban dock. The walk to the castle was deterring many people with only a few hours to spend on the island from visiting it, and a link between the castle and pier was needed. A carriage drive to the castle dating from the 1850s had never been used because of kirk obduracy over the sale of a small parcel of land, and this drive was surveyed as a potential route for a miniature railway.

After a colossal amount of work to clear decades of rhododendron growth, to install drainage schemes and to lay track, the 260mm (10¼in) line was formally opened in 1984 by Chris Green, then head of ScotRail. The journey begins with glorious views over the Sound of Mull towards Ben Nevis before the avenue of rhododendrons is entered, with a stop halfway along for the engine to take water.

The railway has three steam engines, including a

With the Sound of Mull as the backdrop, 2-6-4 tank Lady of the Isles *ambles along the Mull Railway towards Torosay Castle. The engine was built by Roger Marsh in 1981.*

MULL RAILWAY

Length of line: *2km (1¼ miles)*
Operating periods: *Easter–mid October.*
Facilities: *Shop.*
Access for disabled:
  No steps; two compartments for wheelchairs.
Public transport: *Caledonian ferry from Oban.*
Nearby tourist attractions: *Torosay Castle.*
Address:
  Old Pier Station, Craignure,
  Isle of Mull PA65 6AY.
Telephone (information):
  01680 812494 (during operating period)
  01680 300389 (out of season)

On a visit from the Bo'ness & Kinneil Railway, North British Railway J36 No 673 Maude waits to leave Boat of Garten station for Aviemore. The destination board is of NBR pattern.

huge 2-6-4 tank based on a prototype working on the Puffing Billy Railway in Victoria, Australia. The Mull engine can haul 190 passengers in 11 carriages, which is no mean feat for an engine on this gauge.

STRATHSPEY RAILWAY

The Highland Railway (HR) was, and remains, one of the most popular of pre-grouping railways. This is partly because of the dramatic scenery through which it passes and the fascinating history of the region, but also because railways that have had to cope

with difficult operating conditions have a particular appeal. Mammoth snowploughs propelled by three engines occasionally worked for days and even weeks at a time to shift snow that threatened to block the line, and sometimes succeeded.

The main line of the HR ran from Perth to Inverness, initially via Grantown and Forres until the direct line between Aviemore and Inverness was opened in 1898. Expresses continued to be routed over the original route for decades, but in 1965 all services over Dava moor were withdrawn, leaving just the Aviemore–Boat of Garten section to provide a link with distilleries along Speyside until that too closed in

Shortly after nationalization, Great North of Scotland Railway D40 4-4-0 No 62264 stands near Boat of Garten North cabin. The two-road GNSR engine shed was to the right.

◀*Aviemore engine shed shortly after the Strathspey Railway gained access. As late as 1957 about 130 men were employed here, but it closed in the early 1960s and became a garage.*

line for services, as well as relaying track into the four-road Aviemore engine shed. The line as far as Boat of Garten reopened in 1978, and the next section on to Broomhill was completed in 1998, with a view to opening the following season.

A major breakthrough in 1997 was an agreement to route SR trains into the vacant platform at Aviemore, allowing simple cross-platform changes between the main line and SR trains. In 1998 the SR became another heritage railway that has been used as part of Britain's rail freight revival: wagons of timber

1969.

The tourist potential of the area around Aviemore, which has been developed as a winter sports centre as well as a summer resort, provided an encouraging background to the proposal to reopen part of the old Highland main line. The Strathspey Railway (SR) was formed in 1971 and began the task of preparing the

STRATHSPEY RAILWAY

Length of line: *8.8km (5½ miles)*
Operating periods:
   Weekends early April–late October;
   daily early June–September.
Facilities: *Buffet, shops, museum.*
Access for disabled: *Access at stations.*
Public transport: *Aviemore station.*
Nearby tourist attractions:
   Loch Garten Nature Reserve,
   Landmark Visitor Centre.
Address:
   Aviemore Speyside Station, Dalfaber Road,
   Aviemore, Inverness-shire PH22 1PY.
Telephone (information):
   01479 810725
Telephone (locomotive workings):
   01479 831692

from Thurso have been taken to Boat of Garten for the nearby BSW sawmill.

Leaving Aviemore, SR trains run parallel with the main line to Inverness before veering east past the 1897–8 engine shed on the right and the reconstructed signal cabin (as the HR referred to signal boxes) from Garve West on the left. The railway runs through well-wooded country of silver birch, Scots pine, rowan and larch, with views to the right over the Cairngorm mountains.

Boat of Garten was an important junction between the HR and the Great North of Scotland Railway (GNSR), which ran the railway through Speyside to Elgin and Keith. Three platforms were provided and the GNSR had a two-road engine shed, which closed

in 1958. Both signal cabins at Boat of Garten survived to be restored by the SR.

The section on to Broomhill required the replacement of a bridge across the road to Nethy Bridge. In the distance to the east is Abernethy Forest, from where a 610mm (2ft) gauge railway was built during the First World War to convey timber to a loading bank at Aviemore station. Happily timber traffic looks set to provide the SR with an unexpected source of income to help fund the next stage of reconstruction on to Grantown-on-Spey.

➤ *Saved by the late WEC Watkinson, LMS 4-6-0 No 5025 has spent most of its preserved life on the Strathspey Railway. It was built by Vulcan Foundry, Newton-le-Willows in 1934.*

CHAPTER 7

NORTHERN IRELAND & THE REPUBLIC OF IRELAND

Ireland has only two heritage railways: Cavan & Leitrim Railway, which began to reopen in 1992, and Foyle Valley Railway, a centre devoted primarily to narrow gauge railways of north–west Ireland.

◀ *County Donegal Railway Joint Committee 2-6-4 tank No 2 Blanche leaves Londonderry (Northern Counties Committee station at Victoria Road).*

◀ *Standing beside the attractive stone engine shed and water tower is the Cavin & Leitrim Railway's Kerr Stuart 0-4-2 saddle tank of 1916.*

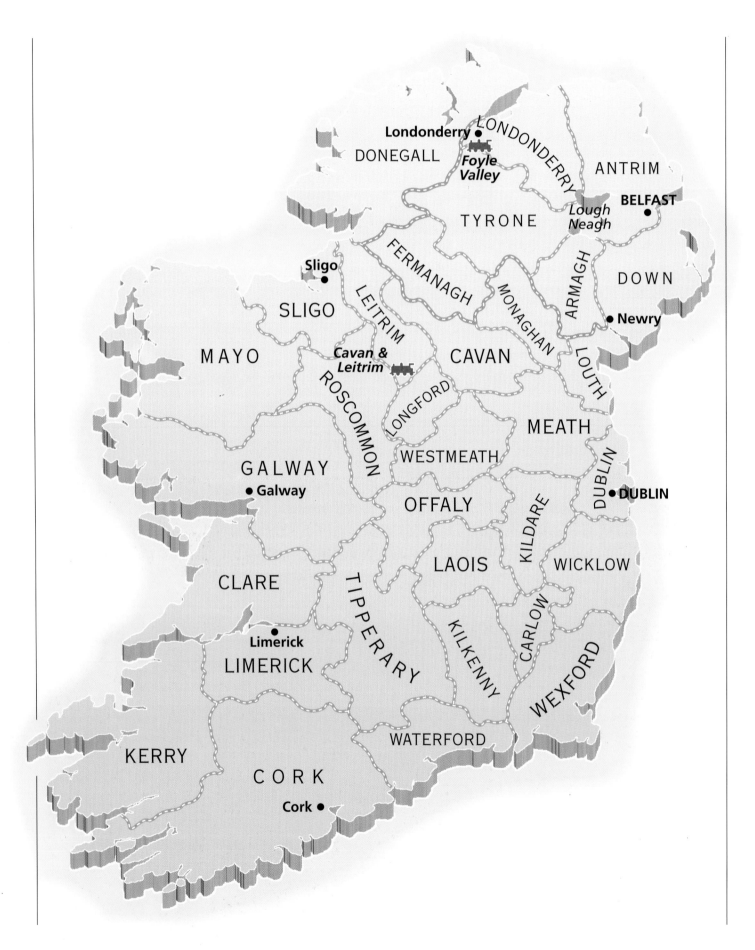

CAVIN & LEITRIM RAILWAY

The Cavin & Leitrim Railway (CLR) was a 77.6-km (48½-mile) system with a principal line between Dromod, on the Mullingar–Sligo main line, and Belturbet, and it opened in 1887. A branch to Arigna for coal traffic opened the following year. The CLR lasted longer than most of the other Irish narrow gauge railways, which were all bar one built to 914mm (3ft) gauge, and closed in 1959.

In 1992 moves began to reopen part of the line, starting from Dromod station. Trains run as far as Clooncolry Halt, and the intention is to rebuild a

☛ *The epitome of the Irish narrow gauge mixed train: an ex-Tralee & Dingle Railway 2-6-0 tank No 3T arrives at Ballinamore Junction from Arigna in August 1957.*

further 9.2km (5¾ miles) to Mohill. Trains are steam-worked at weekends, using a beautifully restored Kerr Stuart 0-4-2 saddle tank of 1916. The engine shed and

---

CAVIN & LEITRIM RAILWAY

Length of line: *0.8km (½ mile)*
Operating periods: *Daily May–October.*
Facilities: *Nearby 'Railway Bar', shop.*
Access for disabled: *Limited.*
Public transport: *Dromod station.*
Address:
   *The Narrow Gauge Station, Station Road,
   Dromod, Co. Leitrim.*
Telephone (information): *078 38599*

⬆ Ex-County Donegal Railways 264 tank Meenglas, which was built by Nasmyth Wilson of Manchester in 1907, is seen here on display at the Foyle Valley Railway Museum.

water tower have been brought back into use, and new workshops and carriage shed constructed. The museum contains a large collection of Irish and British locomotives and rolling stock.

FOYLE VALLEY RAILWAY

Although principally a centre devoted to the narrow gauge railways of north-west Ireland, there is an adjoining operating railway under local council control. The trains are operated by County Donegal Railway Joint Committee (CDRJC) diesel railcars. The CDRJC was the largest of the Irish narrow gauge systems, extending for 199km (124½ miles) at its peak. During the 1930s it developed the use of railcars, using its own workshops at Stranolar, a Strabane coachbuilder and the Great Northern Railway of Ireland's works at Dundalk. Survivors from the CDRJC's fleet operate trains from Waterside station adjacent to the centre.

The museum has two of the fine 2-6-4 tanks built in 1907 for the CDRJC, which were unusual in having outside frames and leaf springs.

➦ *CDRJC tank 2-6-4 at rest by the platform in Londonderry's narrow gauge station, which is being reproduced in part on the site of the broad gauge line at Foyle Road.*

FOYLE VALLEY RAILWAY

Length of line: *4km (2½ miles)*
Operating periods:
  Tuesday–Saturday, April–September.
Facilities: *Shop, museum.*
Access for disabled: *Yes.*
Public transport: *Londonderry station.*
Address:
  Foyle Road, Londonderry BT48 6AQ.
Telephone (information): *01504 265358*

VOLUNTEERS

Volunteers are the very lifeblood of many charitable organizations, and heritage railways are no exception. The broad and enduring appeal of locomotives ensures a diverse array of passionate and committed supporters.

Heritage railways, in common with many charitable or semi-charitable organizations, could not survive without the dedicated help of their volunteers. It is estimated that about 23,000 people volunteer their services to help on heritage railways. This may sound an enormous number, but some of the volunteers may be able to manage only one or two days a year, and the larger railways need 'front-of-line' staff reaching into three figures on summer weekends.

In addition there is all the work going on behind the scenes: overhauling locomotives and carriages for service the following year; repairing the many structures on the railway; looking after and relaying the track; maintaining and upgrading signalling equipment to increase capacity or simplify shunting movements; marketing and publicizing the railway – to mention but a few of the necessary tasks.

It is thanks principally to the innate fascination of the steam locomotive and the steam railway as a whole, including the attractive stations, mechanical signalling and historic carriages, that heritage railways have been able to attract so many volunteers from all walks of life. For many, part of the appeal is the unique sense of camaraderie that springs from a common cause. For others, it is a safety valve to do something at the weekend totally different from their work. Some people relish the challenge of a specific and unusual project, such as the celebrated task of building the Deviation Tunnel on the Ffestiniog Railway: 'Deviationists' from all walks of life, some with no

◀ The allure of the footplate is the reason for many to become involved with heritage railways. Here Tanfield Railway 0-4-0 tank **Wellington** *heads up the hill to Andrews House.*

special interest in railways, relished the prospect of hard labour in an incomparably dramatic setting.

Railways with large locomotive and carriage workshops have realized the vital importance of passing on the skills of the steam age. Those who can remember such complex tasks as the valve setting on a four-cylinder Great Western engine are growing fewer by the year. Many machine tools were developed specially for the repair of steam locomotives, and some training is required for their use. Thankfully there are people young enough not to remember British Railways' steam who are glad to abjure computer games and discover how a locomotive works, or how to restore wood panelling in a coach.

➥ The sight and sound of a steam engine hard at work is probably the most appealing experience produced by any mechanical creation. It continues to attract young and old alike.

The age profile of volunteers on preserved railways needs to be lowered, and most managers are vigorously addressing the challenge. Signalmen as young as 18 are being passed out, and there is no doubt that many young people find volunteering great fun once they have discovered the right niche.

Most railways have a volunteer liaison officer (and sometimes an assistant – the Severn Valley Railway has over 1,200 volunteers on its books), who makes sure that the wishes and aptitudes of volunteers are suitably matched with a congenial role. The liaison officer helps to introduce new volunteers to the old hands, and makes sure they settle in. Many railways hold Open Days, when all departments are open with people on hand to talk about their work. This gives prospective volunteers a chance to see where their interests and skills might best be focused. A typical range of departments might be:

Permanent way
Buildings/structures
Station gardens
Signals and telecommunications
Locomotive
Carriage and wagon
Traffic
Catering

Many preserved railways have high quality magazines that keep members informed of developments in all aspects of the railway and its history. Most railways have a programme of social events. The Severn Valley Railway, for example, holds meetings in Bridgnorth, Bristol, Kidderminster, London, Macclesfield, Stourbridge and Wolverhampton, while the Swanage Railway even has an Aberdeen Group!

➥ *The role of signalmen is vital to the safe operation of heritage railways, and is another popular role for volunteers. Instruction courses are run by Kidderminster Railway Museum, among others.*

▸ *Awaiting the 'right away' with 31,500lb of tractive effort at your disposal is an exhilarating prospect. Drivers invariably come up 'through the ranks' of fireman and even cleaner.*

INDEX

PICTURE ACKNOWLEDGEMENTS

David C. Rodgers: *Title page, 37, 96, 118, 125, 143, 156, 158, 161, 177, 178-179, 190, 191, 192-193, 199, 208, 209, 212-213, 214, 217, 220-221, 251,* **Malcolm E. Ranieri, FRPS:** *6,7 14, 29t, 30, 34, 35, 40, 52, 60, 63, 64-65, 66, 68, 82, 89, 92, 93, 95, 106, 108, 111, 120, 126-127, 145, 146, 149, 150, 151, 176, 185, 204-205, 211, 226, 235, 236,* **S & O Mathews:** *15, 33, 42, 49, 128, 152, 160,* **Anthony J. Lambert:** *8, 9, 25, 27, 28, 29b, 31b, 39, 44, 46, 51, 59, 72, 75, 100, 110, 116, 135, 141, 147, 153, 170, 171, 188, 189, 196, 203, 206, 215, 223, 229, 233, 237, 242, 242-243, 250, 252, 253,* **John Titlow:** *10-11, 17, 61, 73, 74, 81, 112-113, 232,* **Mike Esau:** *12, 13, 18, 19, 20, 22, 26, 36, 43, 48, 57, 58, 67, 69, 80, 85, 86-87, 91, 99, 115, 122, 139, 148, 154, 157, 164, 166, 169, 194-195, 218,* **John Hubbard:** *23,* **Millbrook House Limited:** *31, 32, 56, 78, 88, 102, 105, 109, 119, 124, 129, 132, 135, 140, 142, 159, 180, 200, 201, 224, 241, 244, 249, (P. B. Whitehouse) 62, 79, 107, 117, 123, 133, 155, 247, (Hugh Ballantyne) 24, 38, 50, 70, 71, 83, 90, 162-163, 168, 173, 182, 184, 198, 202, 210, (Peter J. Howard) 45, 197, (David S. Fish) 76,* **The National Trust Photographic Library:** *(L. A. Sparrow) 53, (Nick Meers) 84, (Magnus Rew) 94, (Joe Cornish) 131, (Rupert Truman) 172, (Michael Caldwell) 181, (Matthew Antrobus) 219,* **Ian Bowskill:** *55,* **Neville R. Knight:** *77, 225,* **C. M. Whitehouse:** *97, 101, 104, 114, 121, 134, 136-137, 138, 165, 183, 187, 222,* **D. W. Holroyde:** *103, 207, 245, 248,* **Milepost 92½:** *130, (Melvyn Hopwood) 238,* **Brian Dobbs:** *174-175, 230, 231, 239, 240,* **Mike J. Squire:** *227, 228*